MERELY MOTHERING AND OTHER MYTHS

JANET JENSEN AND GAYLE PETERSON

SHADOW MOUNTAIN
Salt Lake City, Utah

Poem "Encounter" used by permission of the author.

Printed in the United States of America

Shadow Mountain is an imprint of Deseret Book Company,
P.O. Box 30178, Salt Lake City, Utah 84130

First printing September 1987

Library of Congress Cataloging-in-Publication Data

Jensen, Janet.
Merely mothering—and other myths.

Bibliography: p.
Includes index.
1. Mothers—United States. 2. Housewives—United States. I. Peterson, Gayle. II. Title.
HQ759.J27 1987 305.4'2 87-19966
ISBN 0-87579-090-9

Contents

Preface

It was a day of confusion, it was a day of order. It was a time of emotion, it was a time of reason. It was an age of humanism, it was an age of "me-ism." In the words of Charles Dickens, "It was the best of times, it was the worst of times." And it was during this time that two ordinary women got together to write a book—a book about us, about being women and being mothers. And since we are at home, this book is especially *about being mothers at home.*

Gayle is thirty-seven and Janet is thirty-eight. That should tell you something—that we emerged out of the sixties, an era of rebellion, into the seventies where sixties ideals were practiced, and on into the eighties, the forward decade of computers and musical hits such as "Material Girl."

Gayle was raised in Las Vegas in an affluent family of four. She and her older brother were both adopted and their mother stayed at home. Janet came from a contrasting background. She was raised in Alaska in a family of ten. The oldest child, Janet was responsible for much of the child care because her stepmother usually worked outside the home as the family struggled to make ends meet.

But that is where the contrasts end. Somehow, through the years, we discovered (or maybe it was inborn) a great love for children and a strong devotion to them. Are we ordinary? Completely! We see such love and devotion over and over again in our experiences with friends and strangers. But is there a voice for us?

This is a confusing era for women. Even those in the forefront of women's liberation are changing their minds about women's roles. Young mothers, torn between being in the work force and spending their days with their children, are especially perplexed.

This book focuses on a choice closest to the heartstrings of many women, that of being a mother at home. Today, that choice is being lost by many due to the perpetuation of certain negative and inaccurate myths about the mother in the home. We will expose these myths and present a more honest and accurate portrayal of the modern woman.

As experienced mothers, we offer a positive book for all women who are making critical choices in their lives as mothers. Between the two of us, we have lived through divorce and single motherhood, and we are mothers of sixteen natural, adopted, and step-children. We have been poor and affluent, with little and higher education. We have worked outside the home as well as made deliberate choices to stay home. And through it all, we profoundly agree that our greatest accomplishments and sweetest joys have been as mothers at home.

Although we support equality in pay, hiring, and work opportunities for women, we feel the most important changes in our society need to be directed at securing appreciation, recognition, and acceptance of women who are at home. Appreciation for service, love, and relationships needs to be more visible in our culture if we are to enhance the quality of life for the mother in the home.

As mothers at home, we hear many comments that make us chuckle. One frequent question is, *"Don't those kids drive you crazy?"* We look at each other as if to ask, "Do you think we're crazy and don't know it?" We tease each other, but the subconscious message of the question is not lost. Actually, the fact that we have sixteen children between us provides the real laugh.

Other comments include: *"You should make something of yourself."*

"Gee, I thought I was something. If I'm not something, could I be nothing?"

"How can you stand to be at home all day?" We try to make home pleasant for ourselves and the others who live there. However, this often includes a lot of running around. It's hard to be home all day, even when we try.

"Do you work?" That one is our favorite, although we never quite know how to answer. Usually we lie and say, "No, we just sit around the house and nibble on chocolates."

Now, if we heard comments like these on a regular basis, we could become angry. But when they come from good friends, they only serve to spice up life a little. Sometimes we even try to figure out where these statements come from. Are they a symptom of coaching? Are they confined to the unique characters we meet? We don't think so.

We finally decided that these faulty concepts about modern mothers were popular misconceptions vocalized into unwritten scripts that were becoming part of our culture. They continue to exist because few mothers take the time to answer them. One day, on an early morning jog, we decided to put these myths to rest.

We had one advantage that the typical housewife and mother of several children doesn't have. Janet's husband, Larry, is a psychologist, and since he publishes regularly, we thought he might as well help us publish something useful. It didn't take long to convince him that what we wanted to say was as significant as what he was writing. We were even more fortunate in that Larry has been publishing in the area of parenting, and teaching a sex-roles class. Because he has been doing research in these fields, he had a lot of information at his disposal that he has generously shared with us. From this information, we identified ten myths that needed to be answered.

We have taken these myths, which are discouraging and detrimental to the mother at home, and replaced them with positive concepts and aspirations. It is our desire to strengthen the mother at home and give an enlightened perception of her value to her family as well as society.

Encounter

by Ellen Bryson Remington

A learned friend from time gone by
When my pursuits were intellectual
Crossed my path today; and glancing
Quickly at my rounded middle,
Noting the smudges there from little hands,
The wrinkles, too, from childish tears,
He asked, "What are you into now?"

I wish I could have made him understand,
"I'm into graphic arts—a type
Advanced beyond the popular conception.
I deal in shapes so intricate, so exquisite
That in this life I'll never know their limits."

I thought how every day I shape so many things:
I shape the edges of a pie,
I shape a diaper to the tiny legs,
I shape some flowers from our small backyard
The covers on a bed till they are
Soft and welcoming.
I shape small eager hands around a ball
And show them how to throw.

But also with my mind and with my love
I shape the tense and troubled hours;

I take them formless, dark, and shape them
Into light and warmth for spirits' growing.
I guide a pliant, loving mind
Now fresh and good from God,
I try to show him things our Savior would.

I shape the design of his temperament,
The pattern of his moods,
I shape desires in his heart
Of this world and another.

And now in me another life is shaped—
The way he'll look and stand,
The contours of his hands—
And God is partner to that shaping.

Let those who do not understand
Think I'm lost in Merely Mothering.
I smile—and shape my daily chores
Into eternal joy.

Myth 1

The Woman at Home Is Not Liberated

We emerged from that never-to-be-forgotten era of the sixties: an era of internal conflicts, open rebellion, protest marches, changing morality, personal freedoms, radicalism, and demonstration.

Nearly two decades have passed. What messages for women have been precipitated by the turmoil? Do these messages accurately represent the woman emerging in the eighties? What directions—what options—can a woman look for as she begins to know herself and to be true to her innate needs?

Women today have more choices and freedoms than ever before. And so there is an even greater need for truth and accuracy. Some current stereotypes of the mother at home discredit the woman of the eighties. Many paint a negative image of the mother at home. There are still many people who share author Anne Oakley's opinion that "women's domesticity is a circle of learned deprivation and induced subjugation; a circle decisively centered on family life."[1]

If this is true, what is left for the woman who spends a third of her life with her family at home? Is there truth to the belief that the woman at home is deprived, unhappy, and subjugated? Not by our standards! Nor is this belief held by those who have done their homework.

Challenging the Myth

Cheri Loveless, founder of the Mothers at Home support group and publisher of *Welcome Home*, receives hundreds of letters and phone calls monthly from mothers. "One of the hardest stereotypes to stomach," says Cheri, "is that staying at home somehow stunts a woman's personal growth. The opposite is true for anyone who knows how to look for opportunity."[2]

This book focuses on the opportunities available to women who choose to stay home. The challenge of showing this choice to be meaningful for today's woman will be covered in three areas: opportunity for self-development, a focus on education, and the value of contributing to a peaceful society.

Is Motherhood a Profession?

Erma Bombeck, in her book title *Motherhood: The Second Oldest Profession*, implied something mothers innately know—that motherhood is a profession! But is mothering more than a profession?

A profession, according to the dictionary, is "a vocation or occupation requiring advanced training." We know, of course, that a woman needs no advanced training to bear children, although many seek education. But the term *mothering* implies much more. To some, it may well be an occupation or profession. To us it is even greater: it is not just our work, but our life. It transcends a profession or role we play. Motherhood, to us, connotes love, character, patience, sacrifice, dedication, service, and qualities for which no person or institution can give training or degrees. Robert Frost was a writer, but he was more. He was an artist, a poet. Likewise, mothering is our profession, but it is more. Motherhood is a calling, springing from a source deep within us.

Liberating Mothers

Some people believe that society should be organized such that men and women share equally in all aspects of life. The Israeli kibbutz, set up with this goal in mind, soon evolved into the more traditional acceptance of male and female roles. In this social experiment, men and women were originally to labor equally in the workplace and fields; child care was to be done on a communal level. Both sexes were to participate in child care and also in laundry, cooking, cleaning, and other domestic services. But from the very beginning these divisions of labor were somehow hard to keep. Gradually they eroded, until a natural evolution resulted in a predominance of women in the domestic work and child care, while the physically oriented work in the fields and industrial cities became male dominated.[3]

Why the shift toward traditional roles, as happened in Israel? Is it not possible that women *prefer* child care to other work? We think so. And this seems even more likely to be true of women caring for their own children.

The experience of other cultures seems to demonstrate that women would fall into traditional roles if given that choice. For example, Hedrick Smith, in *The Russians*, states that the greatest tragedy for most urban Russian women is not being able to be mothers at home.[4] Another author, Fox Butterfield, in *China: Alive in the Bitter Sea*, noted: "The imperative for women to work in China, ironically, has created a strong countercurrent of anti-women's liberation feeling among some educated Chinese women, much the same segment of well-educated, affluent women who in America have been the most active feminists and for whom a career is panacea. Where the Americans are rebelling against having to be housewives, the Chinese are unhappy about having to be breadwinners. Having a career, once it becomes necessity, can be transformed from a means to self-fulfillment and independence into drudgery."[5]

What the women of these cultures seem to be saying is that there is a natural preference among women for homemaking and child care. Alice Rossie, former president of the American Sociological Association, indicates that there is a predisposition in the female toward some behaviors or abilities such as "empathy, affiliation [or association], sensitivity to nonverbal cues."[6] The female combination of sensitivity to sound and face and rapid processing of peripheral information implies a quicker judgment, commonly labeled as "female intuition." Rossie's disappointment is that no ideology, including feminism, has provided us with a greater understanding of the female sex.

Liberating women doesn't mean changing women or putting them in traditionally male jobs. True liberation is providing choice and opportunity, but opportunities compatible with our basic biological nature as women. When this happens, there will be no myth that the woman at home with her children is not liberated.

Even Betty Friedan, a champion of the movement for women's option to choose a "man's world," has rethought some of her revolutionary platform. She says in her later book, *The Second Stage*, women today "have begun to realize that a little dependence is nothing to be afraid of, and that they won't drown in it—they wouldn't have to drive themselves so hard if they let themselves have those feelings once in a while. And they have also begun to see that those young men are just as afraid as they are—maybe more afraid. . . . "[7] Liberation should include a woman's freedom to choose traditional female role preferences.

In a wise restatement of her values, Friedan actually calls for a "second" revolution in which men and women work together with a special emphasis on the rewards and joys that women receive through their mothering roles. Her enlargement of the feminist position is a fortunate move, in view of most women's feelings. Most women do prefer, during a significant part of adult life, to be mothers at home.

The Mother's Choice

Many employed women, when asked to move into higher executive positions, the career-oriented positions that demand the longer-term commitments, have declined. Professional women often prefer to leave themselves open for the option of staying home part of the time with young children. This, of course, hinders them from moving up the career ladder.

Cheri Loveless concludes that a substantial percentage of working mothers in full-time careers would like to do as well in their parenting as they are doing in their employment. They "openly discuss their desires for more understanding employers during the mothering years." Other mothers drop to part-time work and some simply make the choice to come home despite loss of opportunity and money. According to Loveless, these mothers are not *forced* home; they are making a conscious *choice*:

"The mothers who are solving this 'juggling act' by returning home are totally misunderstood by most of the media. They are an entirely new generation than the supposedly 'stuck at home' group. These women grew up with the women's movement. Gloria Steinem represents history to them, not current struggles. These younger women have always felt free to choose careers, and for the most part were encouraged during their college years to delay family and pursue careers. These women are aware that they have many options, but they are consciously choosing home and family as their first priority.

"Now the fact that so many women are wanting to return home seems to frighten extreme feminists. Somehow they think that a movement of women going back to the homefront would negate recent progress in the 'liberation' of women. What they fail to realize is that the very fact that these women are feeling confident enough to make a criticized choice is evidence that women feel liberated."[8]

Arlene Cardozo, author of *Woman at Home* and a forerunner in supporting the mother at home, says that feminism, which frees women for the success ethic, clarifies the fact that pursuit of material success requires time, energy, and a singleness of purpose that frequently precludes all else. Women and men who prefer to place human relationships over material matters will desire to pursue a *human* ethic, to be free to share and experience life with those human beings who matter most to them—the family members.[9]

Liberated Mothers Are Speaking Out

Liberated mothers who have consciously chosen home are only beginning to speak out with as clear a voice as some feminists of two decades ago. And society will listen, for many are documenting possible undesirable side effects of recent changes in the family structure.

Parenting workshops are springing up in this country, and experts now advocate parents' getting "back in control" as a necessary method of turning things around. They have had tremendous success in getting both parents into roles that demand time and energy for training young people. Parenting takes quantities of time and unlimited resources, both physical and emotional, and experts have discovered that parents are the best ones to give the time and necessary emotional resources to their own children.

Mothers are returning to their children and bringing fathers with them. But most mothers are realistic enough to see that their returning to the home is more practical and likely than their husbands' turning the majority of their lives to parenting. Also, many of these insightful women realized that the popular notion of throwing away housework for traditional male jobs only launched them into a new kind of slavery—working for somebody else, and performing less challenging tasks with less time for self-development. Many of them had become "liberated" into two full-time jobs: one in and one out of the home.

The Value Revolution

The new liberated woman, the one who feels liberated enough to choose home as her major creative effort, is likely to be in touch with a new value revolution. This liberated mother at home sees beyond her neighbor's priorities of material and social benefits. She looks beyond the surface and sees her children well cared for with her own hands and heart. This liberated mother is freer from social pressures and materialistic influence. She is her own boss and schedules her own time, of which she has more. As Jan A. Treinen, a career mother from Scottsdale, Arizona, who recently came home, said, "Corporations always will be out there to hire us professional women, but these precious years with my daughters will not always be here." After being home for four months, she concluded, "A tremendous burden has been lifted from my shoulders. I can't describe it. I never realized how I lived day to day with the constant worry about where my daughter would be that day, how she would be treated, and what her day involved. I think it sapped so much energy from me—more than I ever knew. I feel so *free* from worry now, so content, happier than I've been in a long time, a full-time mommy—what a great career!"[10]

We see a direction for the "new" woman who makes being at home the first choice in planning her life. We find evidence to dispel myths that have relegated homemakers to second-class status. We can offer suggestions to mothers who wish to participate in the value revolution, a revolution bringing fathers and mothers home again into nurturing roles. We support choices for women, choices that can help women feel in touch with their fundamental nature.

Myth 2

Someone Else Can Parent Your Child

On a daytime talk show several months ago, the guest and host discussed a rent-a-mom service that has recently grown popular in a number of U.S. cities. This babysitting service, with its title, implies that parenting is so easy that a mother can be rented or bought. Has society actually devalued the parenting role so drastically? The myth that someone else can parent your child is becoming more prevalent and must be connected with more accurate information. Actually, there are two points of view to be taken when considering this topic: that of the parent, and, of course, that of the child. We will develop both in this chapter to expose the fallacies of this myth.

I'm Not the Person I Was

What surprised us most about being parents were the "larger-than-life" feelings accompanying the sudden assuming of this role. No books, lectures, or classes can prepare a parent for those huge and wondrous feelings he or she will undoubtedly experience. One mother shares these feelings: "My first child came when I was just nineteen. I had been married only a year and was having a difficult time. The marriage did not look promising. To add a baby to the already insurmountable problems, I knew would either make or break us. But I was so caught up in my newborn; it was the dawning of a new era for me. For the first time in my life, I completely forgot myself to care for someone totally dependent on me for survival."

Another new mother from McCook, Nebraska, tells her story of how parenthood changed her. Throughout her entire pregnancy, she assured everyone at work that she was not a "homebody"; she loved her job and would be back to it within weeks after the baby's birth. Then the child was born and, in her own words, "I immediately fell deeply in love with this small, soft, warm baby. I had no idea she would be so special. As each day of her life passed, I did what seemed impossible. I grew to love her more. I loved everything about her; her clenched fist, her rosebud mouth, her smell, her cry—and my heart felt it would burst with her smile."

Her story became more complicated as she described a feeling common to many employed mothers who have returned home. She became lonely at home for adult conversation, and she also missed the extra money. So within six weeks after the baby's birth she went back to her job. But this young mother had yet another unexpected turn ahead. While at home she missed her job, and yet at work she missed her baby terribly. Young employed mothers often have this experience. This mother became a clock watcher and couldn't wait until breaks when she rushed to call her sitter. She described the following conversation:

" 'Hi, are you guys doing all right?'

" 'Yeah, we're fine. I've just finished feeding her and she's gone back to sleep.'

" 'Okay, just thought I'd call and check.'

"I was too embarrassed to ask the other questions on my mind. Did she blow milk bubbles at you? Has she fussed or smiled? Did she wrinkle up her brow and study her rattle?"

So she came to her final solution: she returned to the home. She concludes, "I do not feel at all that I am making a sacrifice. I *want* to be at home. *I'm not the same person I was before I had children.* I've learned so much about myself through them. I know I am no less of a person because at present I don't have what some people call a 'career.' My life as a homemaker is challenging, rewarding, and fulfilling. What's more, I'm enjoying it. Of course, I grow restless at times, but I know this happens with any job.

"Not too long ago, my daughter, now four years old, ran up to me and said, 'Mommy, I love you more than I can.' It brought tears to my eyes because that's exactly how I feel about her. I don't believe I love my children more than a working mother; but for me, loving them means being there."[1]

The Parent—the Natural Care Giver

It is our belief that the bond between parents and children is incredibly strong. Parents love their children beyond measure, including their weaknesses and faults. Janet said of her three-year-old son: "I love the fact that Kendal is stubborn because I can see in it steadfastness as I struggle to help him turn a weakness into a strength. He'll want something his way totally—no compromises. But he also hiked uphill for over an hour a few months ago, without stopping. His tiny three-year-old legs and stubborn persistence carried him to his goal on the mountain."

Who but a parent can see how a child's weaknesses can be developed into strengths? Who but a parent will care enough to take the time to see that poor habits are relinquished and good habits grown in their place? Who but a parent can see the full picture?

Studies have yet to define the innate and "larger-than-life feelings" parents have for their children. In her book *A Mother's Work*, Deborah Fallows gives the example of having just dropped her son off at a morning play camp. As she was about to drive away, she noticed a little boy of about eight bursting out of the school in tears. His mother turned back and took his hand, looked him in the eyes, and spoke gently but deliberately to him. Within a few minutes, after listening to his mother and trusting in her, he calmly and happily returned to the school. "I'd seen it many times before," Fallows continues, "when a child is overwhelmed or confused by something, there is a distinct way *parents* respond, different from the way I had seen any babysitter or nanny act, however loving or competent she may have been. If that boy had been *my son*, I would have been glad to be there for him, too, at that moment. . . . I think it is important that someone who knows him as well as I do steer him through a potentially troublesome situation."[2]

What she concludes from these and similar situations is that parents will do things for their children that no one else would. Ask a parent if he would cut off an arm for a child, and without hesitation he would answer yes. There is a feeling, a commitment, a love, that goes beyond the rules of the rest of the universe.[3]

Why Baby Contests Make a Mint

Why every mother thinks her child is truly beautiful is a puzzlement. Mothers think that their own children are darling and wonder why other mothers don't notice as well. For example, one mother told of an experience in church: "I sat with my absolutely lovely seven-month-old baby girl with my teenage daughters. Next to us sat a college student and next to her a friend and new mother of another sweet eight-month-old baby girl. Both of us were sitting with our baby girls facing each other. We must have been mentally comparing, and my daughter whispered to me, 'Isn't Pam's baby cute?' 'She is,' I whispered back, 'but mine is beautiful.' A moment or two later, my daughter again whispered, 'Mom, do you want to hear something funny? I just overheard Pam's friend say, "Isn't that baby cute?" and Pam said, "Yes, but my baby is cuter." Imagine that. And I suppose that she *really* thinks so.' "

We have used examples of modern nurturing mothers to illuminate the love of a parent. Every mother understands this. Having spent much time tending other mothers' children, we are the first to admit there is a definite difference between how we feel toward children we have tended and how we feel about and react to our own.

The difference does not rest totally in biology, but in bonding, which begins taking place between a parent and child in the first few months of an infant's life. Those who receive the child near birth are said to have a better opportunity to bond with the child than those who receive an older child. Of course, there are always loving adopters of older children who defy all the rules and establish strong nurturing relationships. But as a general rule, and most mothers would agree, the best caretaker of children is the parent—natural or adoptive—for the parent is the one who truly cares most.

Some psychologists reassure mothers that with quality day care, children will not suffer. Mothers will never lose their position of importance to their children; in the eyes of a child, a mother cannot be replaced. Dr. Pat Nachman, researcher at the New York School for Social Research, has discovered that day-care toddlers do not rely on the care giver for comfort or help or companionship as much as the toddlers of full-time mothers rely on their mothers. Instead, the day-care toddlers call out for "mommy" consistently during play and role play with baby dolls for long periods of time, hugging and nurturing the dolls as if they were themselves.[4]

Jane Goodall, world-renowned anthropologist, has studied behavior patterns of chimpanzees for over twenty-five years. She indicates that the "type of mothering a female chimp exhibits has a great impact on adult behavior in her young. This is also true for humans."

She goes on to say: "During the early years the care and affection of the mother and siblings can lead to a self-confident youngster who is relaxed in relationships with adults. . . . In western society families are no longer there to help bad mothering. We must pay attention to the modern way of child raising and its effect on future relationships."[5]

Can a parent be replaced in the eyes of a child? Never. The professionals are admitting it and we must agree. There is no substitute for the parent. Even if the bonding and closeness have not developed, there is a natural tendency for the child to search out recognition and approval from the parent. Remember the story of the little puppy who goes throughout the barnyard from one animal to the next, asking, "Are you my mommy?" This illustration is not so different from real-life cases that are happening around us.

Does My Child Care That I Am There?

One mother recalls the experience she had as a successful professional woman and a small milestone her son experienced in her absence. She was at her neighbor's home one evening watching her son on a playmate's tricycle, expecting to see him ride with two feet on the ground rather than on the pedals. But he set his feet on the pedals and zoomed off. She said she knew that she had missed all the trial and error, the skips and skids he had experienced along the way to becoming an expert pedaler.

Does a child care whether it's the parent or some other care giver watching? Does it really make a difference to the child? From our experience, we can answer yes, it does. The child seeks and desires approval from the parent from the beginning. From our oldest children (Janet's is eighteen; Gayle's is fifteen) to our youngest, not a day passes that they have not sought us out for attention, approval, or recognition. Children are born needing parents to tell them, "You are somebody and you're important enough for me to take the time to care."

One father expressed the feelings his son had for him through this tender story:

> A few mornings ago, very early, just as day began to light our bedroom, my wife and I were awakened by our littlest boy. He came wide-awake into our bedroom, nudging us, whispering in our ears, wanting to come into our bed. I was grumpy and half-asleep. But I made room for him, grumping sleepily at him to try to hold still. But his feet wouldn't cooperate. They began to wriggle, then his knees, and pretty soon he had his arms over my shoulder and his hot cheeks against my back. I finally rolled over, mumbling, "Can't you hold still? What are you trying to do?"
>
> My little boy looked at me. His eyes shone bright even in the dull morning, and puzzlement was in them. He reached for my cheek. "I was just loving you, Dad," he said, "I was just loving you."
>
> I lay there ashamed. How unwilling to share, to give, and receive! What kind of a father, or teacher, or person was I anyway, to forget so easily who I was, and who others were, and how deep and real our needs are? I looked at my little son. His hands still touched my cheek and his face was close to mine at the edge of the pillow. "You were loving me," I said, gaining time.
>
> "Oh yes, Daddy," he whispered, "always and always!" And he began to wriggle all over with the joy of it, like a small puppy in the arms of his master.
>
> It was a good lesson. I needed it. My little boy, less influenced by the world and its counterfeits, had come to me without guile. He had come for an exchange of love and assurance in the early morning light, wanting to share his unbounded fullness without restriction or condition, and I had chosen sleep in its place. How limited we are in our insight and how quick we are to forget.[6]

Sometimes we do forget how important our parenting role really is to us, to our children, and to society. But in any reflective moment, we conclude that there is nothing greater we can achieve in this life than to be nurturing parents. These well-written words taken from the heart of Deborah Fallows's book are clear on this point: "The most important message I carry . . . is simply this: parents are the most important factor in their children's lives. Whether they are with their children two hours a day or twelve, parents are special to children. They make the biggest difference during their childhoods. They make the most impact on the rest of their lives."[7]

For who but a mother and father can see as great a vision for their own family members? And what child does not instinctively long for the tender arms of the mother? In the words of an eight-year-old boy's essay on "What a Mom Means to a Kid," "If my mom wasn't there when I got home from school, I wouldn't know how to fix dinner—and I wouldn't feel like eating it anyway."

Myth 3

Only Babies Need a Mother

General naiveté and some media have sold many mothers on the idea that their teens would get along without them. After all, millions of teens are said to be just fine without much interaction with their parents. But there are also millions being neglected. Teen drug use and teen suicide are skyrocketing. The myth has been perpetuated that our youth can get along without us; only babies need a mother.

But most responsible parents have found that teenagers need a great deal of time and attention. Teens seek direction in the areas of vocational choices, schooling, religion, sexuality, and learning about their identity. They seek an understanding of their new freedoms and their more mature bodies, and they require help when forming new and different friendships. During adolescence, more than any other time, youth need and want someone to trust and talk to about these issues.

In a compilation and interpretation of many studies, one research article titled "Maternal Employment and Adolescent Development" asked, "Are adolescents affected by the employment of their mothers?" The conclusion: "Based on the results of the studies examined in this review, the answer to this question is a qualified yes, some adolescents under some conditions are affected. . . . At present, it appears that maternal employment might be more likely to result in problems when it takes place in the context of family instability, undesirable peer influences, and lack of maternal supervision.''[1]

A Canadian day-care manager noticed the need for more parenting among adolescents at her center. When discussing the pros and cons of day care, she pointed out that the age group we ought to be most concerned with are the elementary school and adolescent children. She said she used to succumb to the pressure from mothers and enroll older children during the hours after school before their parents got off work. It just didn't work out. The older children were bored and frustrated at the center. She pointed out that for working parents in her community, there is no satisfactory solution for the older children. She felt that the lack of supervision at the older ages is a major factor in producing unhappiness and social problems among youth.

Teens Need More—Not Less of Us

This feeling that adolescents are in need of more parenting rather than less is further illustrated in the following quote from a report published in a 1984 issue of *Psychiatry*: "By any reasonable measure, the middle-class family and middle-class children, adolescents, and youth are in a severely troubled state. . . . Unless marriage and family are revitalized and the quality of parenting is vastly improved, the present rates of emotional disturbances and acting-out behavior among young people may well be the augurs of a future even more beset by them, and of a social order even more corroded and unstable.''[2]

Recognizing that the effects of maternal employment may be indirect, Larry, along with a professor at San Diego State University, administered a questionnaire to students asking them to report on their perception of their home life. Girls whose mothers were unemployed during the students' adolescent years reported their fathers to be happier and more friendly, and they more frequently sought their fathers for emotional comfort. They also perceived less anger, stress, and tension in the home.[3] In our opinion, both the adolescent boy and girl benefit greatly from ample one-on-one interaction and parent involvement. These adolescent years can provide some of the most pronounced and long-lasting positive moments in a young man's or woman's life.

A frustrating but realistic principle that virtually all mothers must endure is that the results of our efforts with our children often take years to be realized and appreciated. A soft-spoken, middle-aged friend and mother of seven recently mentioned that her twenty-five-year-old son had called her that day to thank her for her long hours of labor and dedication to the family. He explained that he was just now beginning to realize how great it was to have his mom there through all the difficult years.

Another mother who gave years of devotion to her family was rewarded in a letter of tribute from her sixteen-year-old daughter that illustrates this point.

> Dear Mom,
>
> Thank you so much for encouraging me tonight. I really do love you, mom! You see, this past weekend I've been so discouraged. I really missed you, more than anyone in the family. You being gone was a big trauma in my life. (What am I gonna do when I leave home?!) I missed having you around so bad. You are just my best friend, mom. I mean, at school I get kinda lonely, because I feel like everyone is too cutzy to talk to me. (Heather goes to work experience almost all day.) And no one really wants to sit by me at lunch. I guess I never really did "fit in." I'm not much like my other two sisters, Shauri or Darci—always having friends call them, and going to visit them. I always have been just a little different. I remember the pain I went through in grade school—I'm sure you remember I was a little

clumzier and not as fast and six inches taller than the kids (and sometimes a teacher or two would be a couple inches shorter) and I didn't have the "spunk" or vivacious liveliness like Shauri, or the thoughtfulness, brains and graciousness like Darci. But, mom, through all that, every time I came home crying after someone had called me a name like too tall Jones, or Deenosaur or after some one would throw rocks at me, or burrs in my hair, or spit at me, you would be there, to kiss my tears away, to hug me, to *share* my hurt feelings. And I'd look at your face when I'd tell you, and it was like you were there—I bet sometimes it hurt you more than me. It was like you knew exactly how I felt, and one of the biggest pains was to see your hurt face. I love you, mom, because you are everything I want to be when I'm your age. . . . (I've gotta say my prayer now like you told me to on the phone.)

With love, your daughter and friend,
Dena Rae

The Question of Employment and "No Effects"

A couple of years ago Janet enrolled in a technical writing class in which the students chose their own topics to research. After class Janet told her husband, who is a psychologist, that she was extremely interested in researching the effects of maternal employment on children. "Your paper won't say what you want," he confided to her soberly, "because writers are reporting that there are few or no effects."

"What?" she asked incredulously, recalling her own experiences of employment and also of being a full-time student with young children. Work outside the home had dramatically affected her life! "What!" she asked again, and then stubbornly finalized her feelings with, "I don't believe it!"

"Well, Janet, come on up to the office and take a look through the textbooks. That's what they're saying."

Janet looked through several adolescent and child development college texts. Over and over, to her surprise, she read statements concluding that studies show little or no difference between children of employed versus non-employed mothers. In fact, some writers were stating the advantages to the child of the employed mother. And so, that very day, she decided to take a closer look at this "no difference" conclusion, which in effect is telling us that children don't need a mother at home.

Janet noticed as she studied that one excellent scholar, Lois Hoffman, was repeatedly quoted. She went directly to her oft-quoted 1979 review and was surprised to find this scholarly review more cautious and conservative than these other writers were indicating. Larry and Janet later examined more recent research reports and used these as a basis for a paper and an article called "Maternal Employment: A Closer Look at a No-Difference Conclusion."[4]

In March 1985, they presented this paper at the annual Parenting Symposium in Chicago, identifying several studies showing negative effects on children associated with employment of the mother. Interestingly, other researchers also reported that just because no differences were noted, it did not mean that no differences existed. The differences caused by maternal employment may be there but simply not discovered, because the researchers looked in the wrong places, studied atypical children, or measured those aspects of a child that are not influenced very much by a mother's absence. All too often, studies that find no differences use children from affluent homes who are enrolled in the few first-class, university-run preschools, and then they use I.Q. scores as a measure of the children's differences. Obviously, these poorly designed studies are not going to find big differences between the children of employed mothers and those whose mothers are not employed outside the home. The researchers at the Chicago symposium concluded that when better-designed studies are conducted, the effects of maternal employment on children and their family life will be shown.

Differences will be found when researchers draw their samples of children from the millions who experience the more common forms of nonmaternal care typical in our society. This would include the children in overcrowded and impersonal day-care centers and the children cared for in private homes. Differences will be found when the researchers study how the child feels as he or she tries to understand loneliness, rejection, lack of tenderness, and fear of older children who bully. Differences will be found when researchers study family experiences. Can a mother who picks up a child at 5:30 P.M. (after having dropped him off eight or ten hours earlier) provide as much in the next three hours of cleaning, meal preparation, clean-up, and bathing before bedtime as the mother who had the opportunity to spend eight more hours with her child?

Will Children of the Employed Mother Be All Right?

We hope that all children of employed mothers will receive good alternative care. These children may develop independence and learn from their working mothers, who bring more of the outside world into the home. But we believe these qualities will result not *because* both parents are working out of the home, but because both parents are filling the needs of children *in spite* of working out of the home.

Our purpose is not to say that full-time employed parents cannot work out solutions to raise emotionally well-adjusted children. However, without adequate studies to reveal the full impact of the recent migration of mothers into the marketplace, we feel society has been asking the wrong questions. Researchers have been asking, "Does it damage the child to take both parents out of the home most of the day?" rather than, "Is it *best* for the child to take both parents out of the home most of the day?"

The studies are simply not telling us what the children are missing, what feelings of loneliness they have unnecessarily felt, or what additional growth experiences they might have received. For example, some children turn out to be very successful adults without formal schooling, but does that mean that formal schooling is not to be recommended? Just because something is possible, it does not necessarily follow that it is desirable.

It is possible, for example, for a woman to be an excellent mother while being employed full-time outside the home, but it involves risks; the "supermom syndrome" or the "role overload complex" are two common dangers. Again, the wrong question is being asked: "Can she do it?" instead of "Should she do it?" Role overload, stress, and unrealistic demands, along with guilt about being away from her children, add up to a big pile to place on a woman.

One author who asked some very direct questions had this story to tell: "Not long ago I found myself seated beside a well-known feminist writer at a dinner party. . . . 'Are you at all concerned,' I inquired over the dessert course, 'that so many career-oriented women seem to have adopted a male value system? I mean, there are a lot of kids these days who seem to be regarded by *both* parents as a secondary priority. Wasn't the movement going to make the system more humane?'

"She nodded. 'That's true. It's very unfortunate.'

" 'Do you address that in your book?'

" 'No.' She paused a moment, distractedly stirring milk into her coffee. 'I don't think that's something we can deal with right now. It's not fair to impose that additional burden on women.' "[5]

This type of thinking prompts us to ask, Who speaks out for the children? What do children feel about their mothers' absence? What research study has asked them?

What Do Children Need?

If we were to describe the optimal home climate, it would include love, a lot of listening, affection, and companionship. What mother-substitute can create this kind of climate?

Psychologist Lee Salk says, "I have spent close to twenty years treating adults, and I discovered that all of the most common problems of people in therapy—the inability to form meaningful relationships, difficulties in being able to love and be loved, problems of hostility and dependency—stemmed from a lack of fulfillment of their needs in the early stages of development. It's really very simple—children desperately need to feel loved."[6]

William and Wendy Dreskin make a most persuasive case in their book *The Day Care Decision*. After two years of running a day-care facility in northern California, they observed: "It was obvious there was a problem inherent in the day care itself, a problem that hung like a dark storm over 'good' and 'bad' day care centers alike. The children were too young to be spending so much time away from their parents. They were like young birds being forced out of the nest and abandoned by their parents before they could fly, their wings undeveloped, unready to carry them into the world. . . . We think that in cases where infants, six weeks old and up, are spending eight to ten hours a day away from their parents in a day care facility, it is likely that the result will be difficulties in adult life—problems in alienation, forming close and lasting relationships, or antisocial behavior directed against themselves or others."[7]

Being There at Critical Times

What is a critical time? Sometimes a person wants to talk right now—not the next day, not five hours later. When you have somebody to talk to at the right moment, you may break down and share honest feelings that cannot be expressed two or three hours later. It's important for the mother to be there at those critical moments in a child's or adolescent's life when the child is ready to talk and share problems. Counseling, listening, consoling, and affection given at the critical times, when the child asks for them, are many times more powerful than futile attempts to recapture a lost moment hours (or years) later.

Some of our most critical moments have been in guiding our often unwilling adolescents. The opportunity to influence the formation of a value system in progress is sometimes a once-in-a-lifetime event. Would any parent be so shortsighted as to think that this could be done at his or her convenience or leisure?

Gayle recently found this especially pertinent as she entered the role of single parent. It didn't seem difficult to provide for the physical needs of her younger children when she found it necessary to return to school. What was glaring was the scope of emotional needs evidenced by the older children as they pushed for identity and independence while adjusting to a new family structure. She found it absolutely critical to be home when the adolescent children were not in school. Continual supervision is required to help children develop lifelong habits of daily performance and appropriate family interaction—things that would not happen spontaneously without the supervision of a conscientious parent.

The mother at home is clearly at an advantage in that she can change her schedule to meet her child's needs as well as her own. The typical employed mother, even with the best of substitute child-care provisions, will still have to do things on a preset schedule almost every day around the home—things that cannot be put off, including purchasing and preparing food, cleaning, buying clothes, paying bills, going to the doctor, and running errands. These tasks are essential. Personal moments of mothering are frequently crowded out. These person-to-person moments postponed, delayed, or eliminated are the real loss. Such a picture is painted by one student who relates the following:

"My mother was a school teacher. She worked until my sister was born. I was ten at the time. I remember the empty feeling in the house when we'd come home from school. Many times we'd go to a friend's. There was such a difference at their house, their mother was there. When my mother came home, she was always busy doing the daily tasks such as cleaning, laundry, and dinner. There wasn't much time for talking or playing. I don't remember much about her.

"The reason I speak of her in the past tense, is that she died of lung cancer right after my eleventh birthday. It bothers me now, more than ever, that I can't remember her. I couldn't tell you her favorite color, food or song. I don't really remember her hobbies or distinct personality traits. I don't feel this is because of my age at the time of her death. I tend to believe the cause was the lack of time spent with her because she worked."

This young woman told us that she felt cheated out of a possible close, secure relationship. Later she told us that she worked full-time putting her husband through school until her second child was born. During that time, she faced many of the same problems her mother had. By the time she got home, it was time to fix dinner and begin other responsibilities. Her daughter, not having seen her all day, would be hanging on her and whining to be picked up. She said, "This was irritating and I'd soon become cross. The feeling in our home was usually one of tension and Laura was often belligerent just for attention." She later stopped working and reported, "I am now unemployed and there is an unmistakable difference in the atmosphere of our home, and in Laura's attitude. She no longer needs to throw tantrums or hit and push to get my attention. She is much more loving and patient, and so am I."

When this issue is discussed in Larry's parenting classes, it is surprising how strong the young people's feelings are on this topic. The following is a typical response:

"When I was in the ninth grade my mom started working. That's when I saw that things began to change around the house. She would get up and leave the house at 7:00 A.M. and we would not usually see her again until 6:30 or 7:00 at night. It started getting so that we hardly ever sat down to a meal as a family. . . .

"It got so that my mom really only did the things that she absolutely had to do because she didn't have time for anything else. In addition to working full-time, she started feeling like she wasn't qualified enough for her job, so she started taking night classes. It was at this point in my life that I noticed a big change in my mother. She still loved and cared about people, but she didn't have the time to do nice things for them that she used to. . . . "

Do our children, young and old, need a mother at home? Our experience as mothers indicates they do. And our teenagers are crying out, "Mothers at home—we need you!"

MYTH 4

Quality Time Takes Less Time

We've all heard the cliché "It's the quality, not the quantity, of time that matters." Sounds so catchy, clever, and reasonable. But the error comes from the implication that if Mom gives her children "quality time," it isn't necessary for her to be with them much of the time. This myth, if true, would imply that it's really not necessary that Mom be home because she can substitute "quality" for "quantity" each day. Does quality time take less time?

Challenging the Myth

The bold truth is that solid human relationships require quantity as well as quality time. Dr. Blaine Porter, a professor of Family Sciences, uses the analogy of receiving a delicious quarter-inch steak at a restaurant. No matter how great that steak is, it's still just a quarter-inch. "Give your children your most priceless gifts—you and your time," states Porter.[1]

At a parenting conference a young professional mother expressed the feeling that even though her son is without her much of the day, at least when she is there, her time with him is "quality." She gave the example of the stay-at-home moms she always sees visiting together in the park at a distance from where their children play. She said that when she goes to the park she always spends time with her son pushing him on the swing or merry-go-round rather than passively sitting or chatting as the stay-at-home moms do.

We immediately pictured ourselves in that situation and asked, "What would I be doing? Am I passively or actively involved as my preschoolers romp the playground?"

We found that the answer would depend on the child's needs that day. The employed mother or full-time student mother might spend every free hour trying to capture moments of quality time. She is there for her children, not as a stay-at-home mom, but still as often as she can. She is the mom at the park, pushing them, cheering every feat. This is similar to how a single parent reacts when he or she has custody or visitation rights. Somehow, time with the child becomes more valuable—or at least more intense. Every minute must count. The child feels it and the parent knows that now is the time to influence, to love, to teach—to push it all into that clump of time available and make it all happen.

But time has a different meaning to a mother at home. To understand this difficult concept about time, consider the following account written by a professional woman when she was at home.

"Before I worked full-time, we had loved our daily outings. They were our formless, shapeless, improvised times together when we'd be directed only by the weather or our own moods and energy. Sometimes we'd take a very slow walk down the street to the firehouse to visit our friendly firemen. Sometimes we'd build a blanket fort over the card table and read inside it. Sometimes we'd bake cakes and make a complete mess. I remember that these activities would go on for very long times—certainly at a slower pace and more drawn-out duration than an adult would direct, but one that seemed in keeping with the orchestration of a child."[2]

Sometimes we read research findings that suggest employed mothers spend as much time with their children as nonemployed mothers, and that the time an employed mother gives her children is of higher quality. Deborah Fallows found a startling conclusion after examining the oft-quoted 1982 publication of the National Research Council's Report, "Families That Work: Children in a Changing World." The employed mothers spent only fifty percent less time with their children, according to the report. But the researchers, for the purposes of their study, measured only undisturbed, putting-the-puzzle-together time, while every other real-life activity, such as taking the child to the grocery store or making dinner as the child set the table, did not count. Most parents realize that although concentrated playtime is valuable, many other unplanned activities can be equally important. If we read with our children, that time "counts"; but if we talk with them while in the kitchen, car, or yard, does that time not "count"? As Fallows concludes, "It is hard to tell which of these kinds of contacts has been more important to the children's development or in our sense of a bond with them. I would hate to give up either of them."[3]

Quality Time Comes from Quantity

You need a minimum of quantity time to have quality time. It seems absurd to conclude that if a child gets ten minutes of quality care every day it does not matter if he or she is left alone in a poor environment the rest of the day. Instead, the main point is that quality time requires a certain amount of quantity. And nobody knows precisely how much that is. Sometimes having the hours is just not enough, because you also have to muster up the emotional energy to focus on the children.

Joan Beck captures the irony of the quality time myth in her article, "Mom's Time: Too Important to Waste on Kids." She writes, "The notion that mothers can short-cut child care, even in the early years of an offspring's life, is essential to women's demands for full and equal participation in the work force. . . . " She states that all over the country, millions of babies, toddlers, and preschoolers are waiting at the sitter's house and in day-care homes, waiting for parents to come and take them out for some quality time, not knowing that it's going to be the end of the day when fathers are too tired and mothers too preoccupied. She states, "I don't understand why it's only used for small children . . . why can't you say to your boss, for example, 'I won't be in the office very much this week, but instead of quantity time, you'll be getting quality time when I am in.' " She points out the absurdity of the quality time myth by saying that "maybe teachers could turn their students loose after only an hour of quality time instead of keeping them there the whole day. Or, maybe if a waitress does a quality job of serving the appetizers and salad, you won't object if she skipped bringing you the entree and dessert. Or, maybe if a bus driver gives you a quality ride, he need only take you a fraction of the distance you intended to go."[4]

Professor Amitai Etzioni, a sociologist at George Washington University, comments that the belief that quality time can substitute for quantity time is, in his judgment, ill-founded. One obtains quality time only when there is a sufficient quantity of time. Mom cannot suddenly say to Johnny, "I have five minutes before my next appointment. Let's relate now." He humorously states, "It's getting to the point now where some parents even substitute a 'quality phone call.' "[5]

One father-student tells of his experience of quality versus quantity time:

"Having been in the military I was called on to travel away from home for lengthy periods of time. I soon discovered a lack of time with the children and decided that I would spend 'quality' time with them during the hours we did have together. I planned a lot of activities and trips to zoos and museums these times but usually I had to persuade them to go, interrupt their plans or make a point of how great these times would be. . . .

"Now I'm in college again and working and have a minimum number of hours at home, but I am home every night for family prayer before they go to bed and there in the morning when they wake up. We don't go as many places but we talk a lot more and play football and ride bicycles. Most of all, they know that whatever happens, I'm there each day and they can sit on my lap, talk to me or just see me. I rarely miss having a meal with them.

"Many people say they spend quality time and that's more important. For me, I'll take the quantity. I've never had a best friend who I only spent a few *quality* hours with. They were people I spent all kinds of hours with and really got to know personally without a structured activity each time we were together. That's the type of relationship I want to cultivate with my children and I believe it is nurtured through *quantity* time spent together."

Time for Fragile Moments

One mother-writer, because of quantity time, was able to capture a quality moment.

"One warm, sunny summer afternoon when our daughter was only three, I was sitting on our front porch reading the newspaper. She came running towards me, her little chubby legs carrying her as fast as they could. With her dark brown eyes sparkling, she handed me a bunch of bright yellow dandelions. I took them gently, told her they were pretty and hugged her for a special thanks. Then I laid them beside me and started to pick up the newspaper to resume my reading.

" 'Smell them, Mommy,' she pleaded.

"So I picked them up again and smelled them. A broad smile covered her cherub face and then I understood the true value of those dandelions—no longer were they just weeds on my lawn. She scurried off to some other adventure, but I remained sitting and holding the dandelions. How many other times had I neglected to smell the dandelions? I thought to myself. How many other moments which I could have shared with the children or my husband had I casually laid aside, not realizing the true value of these fragile moments?''[6]

In the words of another mother: "I don't have to be a supermom who sews all my kids' clothes (I can't sew), who does all the volunteer work at school (I do my share), who cooks gourmet meals (we eat a lot of spaghetti and chicken). I simply have to be around my children—a lot. . . . What I need is *time* with them—in quantity, not 'quality.' ''[7]

Relationships take time. And because quality comes from quantity, we need time with our children, in quantity and quality.

MYTH 5

There Is Time to Be Supermom

One woman of our acquaintance, Nancy, is a stay-home mother of two preschoolers. Nancy's husband wondered what she did with all her time. To him it seemed that with only two children, she should be able to keep the house clean and even complete a project or two during the day. But the home was not spotless on his arrival, and a small project every week or two was all she could manage.

One day, after a light chiding from her husband, Nancy proposed a plan. For the next two days she would attend her husband's classes while he stayed home, improving the condition of the house and giving the children "quality time." Anxious to show his wife how to better use her time, he agreed.

For two days Nancy attended her husband's classes, taking impeccable notes and enjoying the change of pace. Her husband, of course, did not fare as well. He found the house difficult to keep up. It seemed that basic child care, as well as the usual unexpected, took more time than he had imagined. And of course, housecleaning took a back seat to the children's needs. At the end of the first day, Nancy's husband had a few excuses as to why the home wasn't shipshape. He also asked Nancy to continue the evening meal preparation, which, of course, she was willing to do. As you might expect, by the end of the second day Nancy's husband had a new appreciation for her role. He even wondered how she managed to find any time for herself.

While some are pointing fingers and asking what we do with all our time, mothers at home are asking, "What time?" After cleaning house, preparing meals, running errands, and giving kids quantity and quality time—there is no time!

Probably the biggest shock we both experienced as young mothers was the loss of personal time. It seemed one feeding ran into the next and endless hours were swallowed into continual care for the baby. Although Janet is the oldest of eight children, and had spent years in child care, no experience, aside from motherhood itself, prepared her for the time-consuming experience of parenting.

Mothers in the home are feeling the lack-of-time-to-get-it-all-done crunch. And mothers outside the home have an even greater dilemma with time. What is the solution? We think it lies in looking at the total perspective, and then in planning.

A Mother's Three Phases of Life

Arlene Cardozo, in her excellent book *Woman at Home*, outlines a woman's three phases of life. She believes a woman raising a family can integrate personal interests and activities into her total life scheme. She feels a woman need not leave home in order to pursue her interests. The woman who achieves balance in her life does not ask whether she should take on activities in addition to raising a family, but rather, when and where to do so. To understand how this is accomplished a mother must see her life as three distinct phases.

The first phase begins with the first child's birth and lasts until the youngest child enters grade school. The second phase is when all the children are in school. The third phase, which can be positive rather than the empty-nest period, starts when the children leave home. Cardozo says that a woman's first phase allows time for building a foundation for herself. She might spend her time primarily at home with children, but a woman can also be involved in different kinds of activities on a day-by-day basis. Cardozo says: "While some women become so involved in personal endeavors at home that they stay there after their last child is in grade school, others find the second phase a time to get involved in activities outside home—in the community, at college, through part-time jobs—which allow the flexibility of being at home after school when their children are there."[1]

She points out that many women in phase three, once the last child leaves home, go full-time to their own schooling or to a job, or move in a direction that they have not tried before. She sums up her findings by saying, "One thing is certain: a woman need not sacrifice one aspect of herself for another. The two major freedoms in being at home are interdependent, rather than independent. One freedom is the opportunity to create a secure home for herself, her husband, and her children, within this vast social order. The other is that while making a home, a woman has the chance to develop and expand her own interests, creative potentials, or personal specialities right there."[2] Women, by recognizing how these phases take place, can plan their lives more optimistically.

Phase One—When Children Are Home All Day

We both are typical examples of the phase one mother. Gayle has one preschooler and Janet, who says she is in extreme phase one, has three. Phase one is usually the most challenging of the phases because the woman is handicapped by the least amount of time. But with consistent planning, mothers can gain small segments of time.

Let us give you some personal examples. For several years Janet was a single parent, in phase two, going to school and working part-time. Then she married Larry and in less than four years had three children, which has thrown her back to phase one again. Realizing which phase she is in helps her to be more patient with life, more accepting of this most challenging phase, and helps her plan for the future. Janet, although sometimes frustrated with her lopsided, home-bound phase, is able, an inch at a time, to squeeze in a little time for herself. For example, in these last five years, she has completed five hours of college credit as well as this book.

Gayle has been in phase one for the past sixteen years. "I hardly know any other life," she says, "but I've always got a plan." Although she worked part-time for a short while after her first baby, she has preferred to be a mother-at-home when one or more children were preschoolers. She is supportive of Janet and the "extreme phase one" situation, recalling the challenges of three at home to be among the more frustrating of times. Having spent most of her undergraduate hours in the field of Child Development and Family Relations, she led her preschoolers in home activities rather than opting for paid preschool, although money was available. She is approaching phase two with the last (and only one) of the six in preschool while she is completing enough college credit for a degree. Over the past years she has taken home study and evening classes sporadically (as time would permit) and has laid plans for phase two and three. "I'm already planning what kind of grandmother I'll be," she says.

We think phase one is a time when mothers can become very despairing unless they keep this phase in the proper perspective. For the mother of the handicapped child, it is more than a phase. This mother needs extra help and support. But for most of us, this phase will pass quickly, even too quickly for some.

One seasoned mother writes, "I was a young impatient mother. I was nineteen when my first was born. She was the sunshine of my life. But I hurried her along. I just couldn't wait to see her crawl and walk. As her pudgy hands reached out for me, I longed for the time when she could talk and we could communicate. Before she was seventeen months, her sister was born, and I was pushing to potty-train. I remember frequently holding and bouncing both of them, hoping to subside potential jealousies.

"When my oldest was two and a half, my third daughter was born. I was not yet twenty-two. This was a difficult and growing-up period for all four of us. But the shock came when, a few years later, the stage was actually over. The bottles, the diapers, the baby talk, and the tender moments only a small child can lend were gone.

"Those stages in my daughters' lives that I had looked forward to, and sometimes pushed ahead, had disappeared into the sunset, leaving only blurred memories.

"Ten years and a new marriage have now brought a different perspective to my daily experience with my youngest children. I look at my four-year-old's strong face and body. Traces of babyhood are no more. And the 'baby' is rapidly diminishing in my two-year-old as well. This time I'm not rushing it.

"Each stage of growth can be exciting, and challenging—each an adventure I desire to savor. I realize this time around that most of what I'm experiencing is moments away from being forgotten. My 'enlightened' outlook helps me to endure the difficult periods with a bit more patience as I enjoy this short season with my little ones."

Phase Two—When Children Go to School

Arlene Cardozo tells about a mother named Marion who is in phase two, with her oldest son in high school and the youngest in grade school. Marion finds this period of growth and development "the most demanding years ever. When the children were little it was fun and games for them. My husband Paul and I always talked and played with them a lot." But now she feels she has four more adults in the household. She says, "When I say 'raising' I don't mean seeing them every so often to tell them a few things. I mean being right there, on the spot, doing what you believe you ought to be doing. It doesn't matter what you tell your children; they won't listen to what you say, but they'll watch what you do!" Cardozo points out that Marion lives what she believes, and she puts "the total family unit before personal considerations."

However, Marion says, "I've always had a penchant for politics, and have been involved in the Democratic party since I was able to vote. When I was home with preschoolers, I kept my hand in politics in the most basic ways. I did whatever I could from home, including licking envelopes (the children helped), calling lists, and typing memos." Since Marion's children have all been in school, she has had even more time for more active political involvement. "I go into headquarters during their school hours, at the height of hectic campaign times, and otherwise work from home between elections." As campaign manager, Marion was responsible for the landslide state senate victory of her friend and neighbor (a woman with grown children). Marion herself has steadily refused to run for office because of the time she feels it would take from her family, saying: "Then I'd be just another do-gooder out saving the world while who knows what goes on at home. This way, I feel I'm able to raise the children and enjoy it and still keep up on the political scene. There's a time for everything, and my time for another full-scale commitment isn't here yet. It will come later on, but right now I want to be on this scene after school and on weekends. The boys will all be grown soon enough—I'm not rushing it!"[3]

Phase two is the period when most of us can start getting involved with activities outside the home. For Marion it was politics. For others it could be PTA and community involvement. For some it will be continuing education. Pursuing hobbies can be a source of satisfaction. But phase two is a period of life to begin planning for your future.

What we would like to stress is that phase two, in particular, is a time for planning and rethinking your priorities. With the children in school, there is a small block of time just for you. What you do with this time should be something to benefit you.

Some women use their time in part-time employment. If a woman is rushing off to a minimum-wage job rather than pursuing the education her heart desires, something is amiss. Even part-time employment can be draining and stressful to the mother and family, especially if it isn't really what a woman wants to do with her time. We see education, a class or two at a time, in or out of the home, as a means of upgrading the quality of life a woman can have. Pursuing hobbies and personal goals can bring vitality and enrichment during these short hours that will add a sense of vigor to your soul and renew your commitment to mothering when the children arrive home, rather than push you into the "role overload" category.

Although equal pay for equal work is an important and necessary standard, most women today still work under men in less-than-desirable circumstances with little advancement in position or pay. We simply feel a woman's time is better spent, if at all possible, in self-improvement so that eventually she will have the marketable skills to enable her to achieve long-range personal goals.

Phase Three—More Time Than Ever

Phase three can be seen as a new lease on life. Women who have put a great deal of effort and energy into the prior phases usually need not worry about an empty nest. Cardozo, who has carefully studied these phases, relieves one possible concern by pointing out that women who build close relationships with their children keep in touch when they reach adulthood. And often they approach their nonfamily employment with a youthful vigor.

One brilliant friend of Gayle's, a mother of eight, decided after raising her own children to start a day-care center, which she runs from her home. Can you imagine? But her business is prosperous and she loves it.

Middle-aged mothers everywhere are plunging themselves into the school systems. One mother, at around age fifty, went back to school and received a master's degree in psychology, then took a job in a family counseling service. "The work," she says, "is rejuvenating. I'm so fresh compared to people who have been doing this twenty and thirty years. A lot of them have lost some optimism by now, many of them are just plain tired of it—but I'm raring to go!"[4]

Life's Sequences

We cannot have everything at once. We cannot be all wife, all mother, all career person, and all public service volunteer at the same time. At one stage you might emphasize career and at another marriage and rearing young children.

Advising his granddaughters on this subject, James Faust eloquently touched the heart of the question: "Sequentially is a big word meaning to do things one at a time at different times. In the Book of Ecclesiastes, it says: 'To every thing there is a season, and a time to every purpose under heaven' (Ecclesiastes 3:1). It seems that the new roles of women have not decreased their responsibility because, while the new roles are challenging, the old roles of wife and mother are in the soul and cry out to be satisfied. . . . Fortunately, women do not have to track a career like a man does. A woman may fit more than one career into the various seasons of life. She cannot sing all of the verses of her song at the same time."[5]

Recently a magazine ran an article about a famous actress who was torn between her motherhood responsibilities and her career. Her interviewer wrote something like this: "When she decides where she is going, there's nothing to stop her from having it all." We as mothers are seeing and feeling the "having it all" pressure. We are told we can have money, marriage, motherhood, travel, and career. But how accurate is this intriguing concept?

We challenge it by saying, "You can do anything you want, but not everything." For the mother, actress, or whatever the role, there are only twenty-four hours in a day. Thus, a mother is forced to set priorities. To be effective, she must decide what is most important to her and begin from there. This is not to say that a mother can't have more than her homemaking role. A mother today can and should have more—but having it *all* is not just an overstatement, it is an impossible and unfair demand.

In her article "Having It All," Sara Davidson comments about forging an identity, building a career, developing a hobby, and rearing a family. She speaks of the woman who is struggling to have it all: "I do not yet understand how a woman can successfully split herself between home and the marketplace. Fifteen years of feminist theory and action have taught us that sacrificing one for the other does not satisfy, but having both together simultaneously is so difficult that no one I know has found anything but the most quirky and incomplete solution. . . .

"The only answer I come up with is that you have it sequentially. At one stage you may emphasize career, and at another, marriage and nurturing young children, and at any point you will be aware of what is missing. If you are lucky you will be able to fit everything in."[6]

Assuming that a woman cannot really have it all, how can she decide what will be of greatest value? Sara Davidson continues her article with a graphic example of such a decision. She describes an encounter she had with three women recently graduated from Yale.

> All three are dark, attractive, lively. Becky wants to earn her doctorate in English, Jan will start medical school in the fall, and Kate has just finished her first year at Columbia Law School. . . . They have been giving serious thought to what they want from their lives. . . .

Jan says, "I know a good marriage will be harder for me to find than a good job. I want to marry a man who's at least as bright as me, who's outstanding at what he does, and who'll go fifty-fifty with me in the house."

The others laugh. "Forget it," Becky says. "Have you met guys who are willing to stay home with children? I have, and I wouldn't want to marry them. I don't think men can become successful men—strong in the world—and still do fifty percent of the female roles."

Kate hits the table. "But women who do the male roles still have to do all the female things. It's unfair, and I *burn* that every man doesn't have to worry about splitting himself."

I ask if they think their lot is better than that of their mothers and grandmothers. They are silent—a telling silence. "Feminism is great as an ideal," Kate says, "but the reality isn't always so pretty."

What is the reality?

"It's holding your best friend's hand while she's having an abortion because she can't pursue her career and have the baby."

"It's crying in the women's bathroom because you're in a male environment and men don't cry."

"It's being successful and being alone because men don't respond that well to assertive women."

"It's running from Columbia Law School to Elizabeth Arden to make yourself beautiful for the handful of men available to women like you."

If you *had* to choose, I say, posing the impossible question, between having a family and having a career, which would you choose?

Instantly the future doctor, lawyer, and English professor say, "Family."[7]

The Nonexistent Supermom

To most women it is frustrating and sometimes intimidating to see those frequent pictures of women who supposedly do it all. Do they really pull it all together? We've all seen her—the superwoman, mother of the year, PTA president, novelist, artist; she bottles jelly and fruit; she makes her family's bedspreads, pillows, and matching curtains; and she raises six kids! It wears us out just writing about it. We have known remarkable women who have seemed to fit the description. But inevitably, in each case, these women have juggled and sacrificed something to do all they do. In other words, we simply do not believe in the superwoman myth. Some of us accomplish more than others. We all have varying circumstances and abilities. We can and should do what we can do, and expect no more. To compare ourselves with only the positive picture of what the superwoman seems to do is self-defeating and demoralizing.

The supermom role is often pushed on a mother with the best of intentions by well-meaning others—even the husband. One husband described how he changed his plans for his wife. He said he was fully prepared to place their child in full-time day care so that his wife could return to work as rapidly as possible. He thought this would be for her own good and for the family's financial well-being. He confessed he believed this action would pass for equality, not to mention progressive thinking. But his wife felt uncomfortable with the pressure—society's and his. Her own powerful sense of what was best for Sadie, their daughter, prevailed. He said, "Though for a time my wife remained at war with herself, and was forced to endure the occasional skirmish with me, that instinct continued to determine the way our child was brought up. And eventually I, too, changed—not so much because I was particularly flexible, but because the evidence before me was irrefutable. . . .

"It may be a trite observation that there is no experience more intensely humanizing, none so apt to put things in perspective, as a couple of years hanging around with a very small child. To be sure, such an experience is frequently trying, and is always exhausting. But for those of us unaccustomed to acknowledging, let alone expressing, what is best within us—especially for those of us who were ourselves bruised in childhood—the experience can trigger a lifetime's worth of pent-up joy. Our days by Sadie's side—virtually all of her mother's and mine whenever I could steal them—were an investment rapidly returned manyfold."[8]

Setting Priorities

One so-called "supermom," mother of five, lecturer, writer, tells of her experience and priorities and how she was surprised to discover that other "supermoms" were struggling as she did. As she walked into a university room to speak, she sensed immediately that several of the women in attendance felt she could not relate with their situations. She was older and the introduction made her sound so illustrious—a person who lectures and writes books. How could she relate to someone who tends babies and cleans house?

After the introduction, she felt she had to break the barrier of superficiality, so she proceeded to share with them the fact that in addition to her teenage children, she had two preschoolers and another little one on the way. She shared her memories of her early married life, when she was helping her husband get through school. She verbalized their worries and then said, "But I must let you know that I have discovered something much more exciting than sculptured nails, gorgeous wardrobes, or exotic cruises. The time spent with your husband and children is what life is all about." She finished her evening by honestly meeting them on their level, as she continued, "The only plus I have over you is that I am older, and hopefully those years have shed some understanding. I must let you know that if I had my life to live over, I would spend even more time with my husband and children, because at last I have begun to reap some of my rewards which are evidence that my efforts were not in vain." She continued by telling them about a teenage son who is the apple of her eye. They have had so much fun joking and laughing with each other. He is tuned in to her feelings, and he tries to help when he senses that she is experiencing a "low." She said that if she had not taken time with him when he was small, they would not have this good relationship now.

She also told of a daughter who means the world to her. To establish good relations with her, she gave up luncheons with the ladies and took her daughter to lunch instead. Now as they run to the store to shop, or sit and visit about life, she is most grateful for the bridge they took the time to build. Lastly she told them about another son. "Barry and I waged a difficult battle to prove that he was every bit as important and outstanding as his older brother and sister." She sacrificed to work with him and can say: "Now as I watch that young man participate in his sports, walking with confidence, there is nothing I would trade for all those hours invested with him in his younger days.

"Being able to reap some of the blessings of staying at home with our children makes me more determined than ever to spend my minutes, hours, and days with our little ones. The sculptured nails, the coiffured hair, the spotless clothes mean nothing when compared to one of your children."[9]

Rule Number 1, 2, 3 . . . Don't Compare

Janet still remembers when, as a young mother of three preschoolers (her oldest not yet three), she was struggling, trying to adjust to a new baby and a lopsided schedule. Her sense of what she could handle prompted her to drop all other obligations outside her home. "What is the problem?" one lady remarked. "You're no different from the rest of us. We have small children, and we're doing it!"

"But I am not you," was her quiet reply. This is a profound truth. Each of us has a different set of circumstances, different children who are different ages, different relationships, different personalities, different metabolisms, different environments. Some of us will accomplish more than others outside the home during our three phases of life with our families. Others will accomplish less. But who can say what is more or less when it comes to building family relationships? We must constantly balance our family's needs with our own. And because our needs mesh into the family's, a balance is automatically created. For, although it seems lopsided (as phase one often does), because our needs are integrated into the needs of our families, we rarely come up empty-handed, even if we have only a few hours a week to pursue our personal interests. When we do feel cheated, we back up and spend some quiet time reevaluating priorities. Remembering that supermom doesn't exist, and keeping track of the phase we are in, helps us to keep in mind our limitations as we sequence and plan our lives to their seasons.

MYTH 6

No Financial Security for Mothers at Home

We have both felt the gnawing of empty purses. Although we have not experienced every woman's financial reality, we've had enough experience to know that financial security is a necessary achievement for the well-being of the family.

Janet spent several years as a single mother with three young children. It was a hard time, as she had no job skills and little child support or help from family.

Several years ago when Gayle's husband was in an automobile accident, close to death for two months, she knew she needed preparation for financial security. He recuperated at home for two more months, and after five operations was only able to work part-time. Although she had some college education in the area of child development, she didn't have anything she could "market" and preferred to be in the home with the four children she had at that time.

These past financial dilemmas have left us in search of ways women can be financially secure without sacrificing family well-being. What options are available to the woman who prefers to be at home?

We are aware that to many, family well-being and financial security are viewed as one and the same. We are also aware that many families must have two breadwinners to provide the necessities of life. But we hope, with this chapter, to introduce insights and support for the best care of our families and our relationships. We will show ways that women at home can find financial security *and* family security. In fact, we boldly assert that the woman at home can be better prepared for the future!

The Scare

Many women are told that if they are not consistently employed, their future financial security will be in jeopardy. We learned of a well-meaning lecturer who has made a career of crusading women to the work force by using frightening statistics. We hope to defuse the fear of women who prefer to be in the home and give them more than a flicker of hope for their financial future.

Because we both have felt the fear of financial insecurity, we have sought to formulate ways to dispel this fear. During the search we came to realize that it is shortsighted to believe that the *only* way to be prepared for financial security is with continual employment outside the home.

It is unfortunate that many women will spend most of their lives in employment that is not self-fulfilling. They feel they must remain employed so that if they really need to be employed they will be qualified. We feel it is not logical to spend your time away from the relationships you value most (your spouse and children) in order to be prepared for the time when you will be without these relationships. Time to develop relationships with children, who too soon are gone, goes by quickly enough without being further squeezed. The working mother also loses time for personal development because after employment, mothering, and housework, there isn't any! Time is a limited commodity. The hours and days spent building memories, communication, and trusting relationships need to be guarded, rather than spent elsewhere. A woman should carefully consider such losses before she leaves the home for unwanted employment to prepare herself for a time when she possibly may be alone. The idea of organizing the precious minutes of a life toward this pessimistic future seems almost morbid!

In the preceding chapter we discussed life's phases and sequencing as an answer to some women's dilemmas over career and mothering. If a woman uses her time wisely while she is at home during the family years, she may actually be better prepared for financial security in the future. In the following sections we will discuss some positive options and what some women are doing to meet future challenges while living the way they want to in the present.

Money Facts

There is much to be said about how to handle finances—perhaps too much. Our goal is not to specify one way over another but to provide insight into some healthy attitudes about the money that flows through families.

A woman's contributions toward the care and keeping of the family and to society through this effort are just as valuable as the salary brought home by the wage earner in the family. In any event, a woman "earns" 50 percent of the income of the family. This can be seen graphically in the case of divorce—usually the judge will award 50 percent of the assets to the wife. Women can benefit from gaining an understanding of their position with regard to legal rights.

A great deal of information is available to the woman who sincerely wants to be financially secure. If such is the case, she *must* become educated as to what her options are. Bonnie Siverd, an author of many financial articles, recently offered some strategies on securing a good financial future. She listed the twelve issues briefly restated here:

1. *Plan Now.* Fear of doing something foolish can paralyze you, but not doing anything is the worst mistake.

If you don't have time to think about finances, set aside a specific time each month for this purpose. Some helpful books include *The Lifetime Book of Money Management* by Grace Weinstein and *Money Talks* by Robert Rosefsky.

2. *Save Regularly.* After fixed expenses, take a look at where the rest of the money is going. You can have your bank pay your savings account automatically from your checking account. Add to the nest egg with raises, extra money from a paid-off loan, or tax refunds.

3. *Set Money Goals.* A financial professional can help you find ways to save for a house, a child's college, retirement, and so on. Start with an emergency fund of "liquid" cash in a money market or savings account (three to four months' worth). From there make conservative investments. For children's education, put money in accounts in their names to reduce taxes. Learn about IRA and other investments.

4. *Recruit a Financial Team.* Banks, brokerage houses, and financial planners sometimes offer free money seminars—you have no obligation to buy. Adult education classes are also available.

5. *Diversify Your Investments.* No single investment meets every financial need. Become educated.

6. *Don't Overpay Your Taxes.* If your tax bracket is 33 percent or above, consider a tax pro. An employee benefits officer can show you how to adjust your exemptions for payroll purposes.

7. *Keep Charge Card Bills Low.* Chronic spenders should leave cards at home for a few months or cut them up. With interest on charge cards around 18 to 21 percent, much income goes for nothing.

8. *Comparison Shop.* Shop for the best prices and the best interest rates when you must finance something. Compare fees for checking accounts, bounced check charges, and services.

9. *Buy the Right Insurance.* You should have life insurance if someone is dependent on your income or if you are

a homemaker with small children who would need a housekeeper if you died. A new form of insurance is now offered called single premium—ask about it. Other types are term, whole life, and group.

10. *Use Common Sense.* Ask about pitfalls of a money decision and think through the consequences. Don't commit too much to one project. Remember, if something is too good to be true, it probably isn't. Never sign anything you do not understand.

11. *Stay Flexible.* No money decision lasts a lifetime. The economy changes and so should some of your investments.

12. *Take Charge.* No one can be guaranteed to take care of you—not your father, husband, or Uncle Sam. Build a credit history for yourself and keep some assets in your own name even if it's only a checking account for emergency use. Be sure you know *all* the details of your finances. "Just because you're a woman, don't hold back," says Washington, D.C., financial planner Robin Oegerle. "The only lasting security is what you build for yourself."[1]

One woman realized how undereducated she was about her financial situation when she filed for divorce in January 1986. She had no life insurance, no idea what their medical insurance was, what their loans amounted to, or anything. She gathered items of information from their files and photocopied them, replacing them shortly before the files were removed. Thus she learned that by the end of 1985 about $100,000 had passed through their bank accounts without any provisions being made for retirement, trusts for children, or savings. She immediately signed up for an adult education class on finance and received, for ten dollars and four evenings, an enormous amount of information about money dynamics and how to make your money grow. Some of the topics included: the importance of saving 10 percent, mutual funds, ratings of stocks, municipal bonds, zero interest coupon bonds, tax-deferred bonds, what capital gains are, various kinds of insurance, the annuities of amounts of money at various interest rates, wills, revokable living wills, trusts, family partnerships, treasury bonds, treasury bills, treasury notes, GNMAs, and others.

With this knowledge, she was able to begin to build financial security on the child support and alimony she received. She now has a three- to five-year plan to be financially independent in the event that her financial sources are adjusted or cut off.

What Some Women Are Doing

Many recent periodicals have highlighted what some women are doing to augment their incomes while remaining with their families. One story that comes to mind is that of Mrs. Fields' Cookies.

Many are well-acquainted with the story of Debbi Fields, who took a look at something America loves—a chocolate chip cookie—and made it into a thirty-million-dollar business by 1983. In 1977 she started talking about opening a store. She asked a lot of experienced businessmen and they said, "Forget it." Her husband was willing enough but found himself worrying about what failure would do to Debbi's self-esteem. The banks could only say, "You want to sell *what*?!" But Debbi persisted and on her first day found she could only sell cookies at the food arcade if she passed out free samples, but she made $50.00. Her husband, Randy, had bet her she wouldn't have $50.00 by the end of the day. The next day he bet her $75.00. She produced exactly that.

Debbi Fields is a mother to Jessica, Jenessa, and Jennifer. After a visit with Debbi in 1984 an interviewer said, "Debbi will sit and talk for a while, then charge off to breast-feed the baby. Her office features a rockabye-baby device with a fringed top." Now she is wife, mother, and owner of a multimillion dollar company.[2]

This type of "homework" has become known as the cottage industry. There are many hobbies and talents that may be considered services and could be money makers. Consider your own interests and talents for such possible cottage industries as: aerobics or dance classes; craft sales; furniture refinishing; antique dealing; resale of children's clothing or baby equipment; wood art; proofreading and editing; correcting papers; telephone answering service; sewing; cleaning; animal breeding and/or pet care; rental property management; catering; meals for shut-ins; art and graphics; computer assistance or lessons; tutoring; day care; typing and resume preparation; bookkeeping; music lessons or singing groups; mailing services; research assistance for special projects; photography; beauty salon—hair or nail treatments; yard or pool care; or anything else you might have a talent or interest in.

While some of these may seem outlandish, there are real needs in some communities for these services. Three such self-sufficient women deserve attention here.

Dorothy was a nurse in World War II who married a handsome pilot. She raised eight wonderful children who are well educated and self-supporting. Dorothy has a natural ability with children and has set up an environment in her lovely home for the operation of a high-quality day-care center. She combines older children who come after school with younger children, thereby teaching the older ones some child-care skills in the process. She does so well that she can hire some of the care to high school students on some afternoons and still make money. She also occasionally takes vacations and leaves the care to college students home for summer work.

Ann is another very successful friend who married at eighteen. She is now in her mid-forties and is a practicing, publishing psychologist in Tacoma. She runs an office in her home. She didn't begin her education until about age thirty-five, when she entered the second phase, as the youngest of her six children approached school age. Ann began by reading and studying and taking classes. Her efforts at further education have helped her children through the university years.

Kristen has three preschoolers still at home, one of whom is handicapped. She was an aerobics instructor and fitness enthusiast before the children came, and had dreamed of having a place of her own. She conceived the idea that students from the nearby university (and anyone) would benefit from aerobics classes if a location could be found. Approaching a local dance hall (complete with lights, mirrors, and music), she was in business: two hours of late-afternoon sessions with as many as a hundred participants. She has arrangements with several local businesses (including the police department) for corporate fitness programs whereby she can offer discounts for their exercise and they benefit from greater productivity.

Saving Is Earning

Many women can contribute a great deal of "unseen" money to the family by becoming educated on how to be better managers. Consider this story from *Welcome Home* about a woman from Omaha, Nebraska, who had a large, unexpected bill to pay.

"The thought that I could work outside the home to bring in extra money did not enter my head. I saw myself as a mother at home and that was that. I just figured I would hold down expenditures for an entire year. . . . Before I went to sleep, I knew what I would do. I would get tough with myself. If we could get along without a particular item during the current week, I would postpone buying it. I mentally crossed some items off my shopping list and slept soundly. I felt equal to the challenge."

As the days went by and she crossed off an item here and there, it tended to also get crossed off in succeeding weeks. She realized she simply hadn't needed many things she had been buying out of habit.

Her shopping habits also changed. She avoided all impulse buying. As she shopped, she listed her purchases in categories (clothing, auto, recreation, and so on). This way, she grew aware of excess. She was motivated to consider what things and activities held long-range value and her debt was paid on time.

Having found that she could save money, she started saving *before* she purchased—thus earning interest while saving for what they wanted, instead of paying out 18 or 20 percent while struggling to pay bills. She later stated: "That experience in saving early in our marriage was a valuable education for me. Even though I did not contribute money to the family income by earning a salary, both my husband and I feel that I contributed a great amount by spending wisely and saving wisely. Perhaps our financial foundation is more solid than it would have been had I been earning and then freely spending. Do I feel like a martyr for having done without some things I might have bought? No way! Having fewer things to store, sort, and discard has made my housekeeping easier. My time spent as financial manager was a stimulating experience which has rewarded us well."[3]

Dual-Employed vs. Dual-Career Marriages

Dual-career marriage is the term given to a relationship in which both partners work outside the home for an income. We think a distinction should be made between women who are involved in enriching careers and those who have low-paying, low-status, inflexible, less-than-challenging jobs. It might be more accurate to describe the latter category as *dual-employed* marriage.

Some research indicates that there is a positive correlation between a woman having a career and her happiness level. But the happiness level of a woman in a dual-employed situation is less than that of the dual-career couple usually held up as an example. In any case, not all experts support the idea that employed women are happier. Let's see what is being said on the other side of this issue.

Conditions that have traditionally held marriages together are altered in a dual-career marriage. These are called "linkages," and they either discourage divorce or actively encourage the continuation of the relationship. Shared activities, such as providing a home, managing common property, and raising children, create bonds. Dual-career couples have less time to spend together in shared activities, and may even hire substitutes to perform some of them.[4] They also have less time for common hobbies and social outings. Bonds such as these form strengths in a marriage—because they are frequently absent for dual-career couples, others must be found.

Other linkages are based on mutual dependency. If partners do not need each other, there is less risk involved in ending the marriage. For example, in a single-career marriage, the wife may depend on her husband for financial security and a social network. Her husband may depend on her to define his role and give him a sense of worth. In a single-career couple, these and many other mutual dependencies may help hold marriages together.

Additional conflicting decisions come up when women who are working ask: "Whose job should we follow?" "Who will take leave to be with a new baby?" "Should we accept my transfer?" Even relatively minor decisions: "Who will fix dinner?" "Who will take the children to the doctor?" "Should we go to his office party or her company dinner?" come up almost every day. These decisions usually arise from conflicting time demands, priorities, and expectations. In an article titled "Real Men Don't Earn Less Than Their Wives," studies are cited showing serious problems among working couples. Incompatible calendars, competing priorities, and differing expectations create most of the daily irritants of dual-career households. The schedules and responsibilities of two professionals are not likely to be simple. Problems around expectations add to the tension. This is especially true if there is a differing attitude about gender roles—"men's work" and "women's work." This may, for example, lead to conflict over who should be responsible for housework and what priority should be placed on spending time doing it.[5]

Similar conflicts crop up in single-career families, of course, but the added element of a wife's professional obligations and accompanying stresses increases their frequency and seriousness in a dual-career household. In order to reduce these conflicts, a couple must be organized, flexible, and explicit about expectations.

Stress

Stress is commonly brought on by change, conflict, and pressure. These occur more abundantly in dual-career relationships. The uncertainties and possibilities for change are doubled when two jobs are considered. When these are added to job-related pressures for both partners, the accumulated stress can be tremendous.

Stressful events can occur at home as well as work. Demands of children, threat of illness, and related worries all produce stress. With two careers, there is little margin for the unexpected, and when it happens, resources may be stretched to the limit.

The results of excessive stress threaten marriage relationships. Tension between partners may run high, causing irritability and making small problems appear unmanageably large. Or, at the other extreme, partners may withdraw from each other in exhaustion, becoming psychologically unavailable to one another.

Role Overload

Marriages in which both partners are employed experience more conflict due to the pressure from traditional sex roles, but also because of role overload. Role overload describes the excess work demands placed on women who must manage both a home and employment. Some believe that women today may be putting in longer hours than their grandmothers did on the rural farm, and at the same time must also work away from the home. Actually, the amount of work done per week by the employed woman with two children varies from seventy-one to eighty-three hours.[6] She spends less time than her nonemployed counterpart on food preparation, housecleaning, and laundry, but perceives that she spends more time because these extra chores are taken out of her leisure time, sleep, and sense of humor and personality.

Marital difficulties seem to spring from fatigue and irritability brought on by role overload.[7] Men whose wives work outside the home perceive that they (the men) do more housework than they actually do.[8] In a more careful study of household task performance, one research team found little evidence that equality was approached.[9]

The importance of this discussion for financial security is expressed in the following conclusion: *When employment contributes to marital instability, it is not giving you financial security.*

Employment and Money to Spend

Even if a homemaker is not concerned about securing her future, she may be concerned about paying the bills that are realities today! Many women are caught in the dilemma of finding employment just to get the family out of a tight spot, believing that taking a job is the only way to provide the necessities for their children. Does employment give you more money to spend?

In an article in the *American Economic Review* it was shown that the working woman will spend up to 50 percent of her income on work-related expenditures. These expenditures obviously will not result in increased financial benefits to the family. Also, most women will find only low-paying jobs. It is estimated that after considering the greater efficiency in producing goods and services at home, and taking into account job-related expenses and additional taxes, the family with the wife working needs about 30 percent more income just to maintain the same standard

Net Income Effects of Additional Employment

I.	Expenses Attributed to Employment	
	Redundant insurance	________
	Increased tax liability (higher tax bracket)	________
	Educational expenses (job-related)	________
	Additional travel expenses	________
	Additional contributions	________
	Meals and snacks at work	________
	Household and child care expenses	________
	Extra clothing and grooming	________
	Total expenses	________
II.	Net Income Before Expenses	
	Gross Earnings	________
	Less:	
	Social Security	________
	Federal Income Tax	________
	State Income Tax	________
	Additional Withholdings	________
	Net Earnings	________
III.	Net Income Effects	
	Net Earnings (Part II)	________
	Less additional expenses (Part I)	________
	Net Additional Income	________

of living.[10] To appreciate the costs of being employed, study the information in the acompanying table, which shows the net effects of additional employment.

Careful consideration must be given to the actual increased spending ability of the family when a woman leaves the home for outside employment. Consider this true story of Mary and Joe, described in a marriage and family textbook.[11]

> Joe manages to keep the family afloat financially until their second child is two and one-half years old.

Mary and Joe realize, especially with the high inflation rate, that they simply aren't going to make it comfortably on his earnings alone. Mary has heard that a local company is expanding and needs new employees. She applies for a job, receives it and suddenly finds herself to be a full-time working mother. Although her income is relatively small compared with Joe's, she believes her $900 a month will not only get them out of debt but will allow them a few luxuries they have had to forgo. Also, she and Joe hope it will allow them to save a little money toward a house down payment.

Unfortunately, Joe and Mary learn that her $900 does not raise the family income by that amount. Before Mary can go to work, arrangements must be made for child care. . . . She decides to leave the children with Mrs. Smith, an older mother down the street, four days a week ($40 per week) and Joe's mother for the remaining day (free). This way the children will be with people they know and will be staying in their own neighborhood as well. If this arrangement doesn't work out, Mary can put them in the day-care center. Thus, Mary's monthly child-care costs are $160. This leaves $740 from her paycheck.

Transportation must be considered. There is a bus that goes past her workplace. The route is circuitous and requires her to leave the house one-half hour earlier than she would have to leave if she drove. Taking the bus both ways will cost an additional hour of time per day plus $22 per month ($1 per day). Riding the bus also means that Joe will have to take the children to the sitter each morning. They decide that buying an older economy car is probably the best solution. With the added car, Mary can help deliver and pick up the children and can be more efficient generally. They borrow $1200 for twenty-four months at 15 percent interest and buy a used car from a friend. The car is in good shape and, other than needing a new set of tires, requires no work. There are additional insurance costs, however. They purchase only liability coverage, thinking that because the car is old, it isn't worth the cost of collision coverage. The total monthly cost for the car is $100. The breakdown is as follows:

Payment	$ 65	Discount interest adds up to $360 for two years. This makes a total debt of $1560. Divide by 24 months to get monthly payments of $65.
Insurance	$ 10	
Gas and maintenance	$ 25	
Total	$100/month	

Subtracting $100 more from Mary's monthly paycheck leaves $640.

Taxes and social security are also deducted from Mary's paycheck. She takes no deductions for the children, and finds that another large bite has been taken from her paycheck. In addition, her income added to Joe's puts the family in a higher overall tax bracket. They will receive a refund at the end of the year because of child-care costs and other deductions, but when all is said and done, the taxes and Social Security costs average about $150 per month. Thus, Mary's monthly check shrinks further to $490.

There are also miscellaneous costs associated with Mary's going to work. She doesn't have as much time for food preparation and household work. She uses more partially prepared foods such as frozen dinners that tend to be more expensive. She also sends more clothing to the laundry. In addition, she has to buy some new clothes to wear to work. These costs add up to about $100 per month. The bottom line is that her $900 per-month pay adds only about $390 to the family income. This amounts to about 43 percent of her gross pay.

More Facts to Consider

According to Dr. Jerald Mason, a financial counselor, the ideas about a "typical" family do not perfectly fit most families, for if the husband's salary is above $20,000 the wife's financial contribution will probably be minimal. The structure of the federal and state income tax rate schedules explains such differences. When a wife earns less than $10,000 the family will receive little financial support from her unless the husband's salary is also low.

A large expense usually incurred is child care. A mother who returns to employment and must pay for child care for more than one child may find that the family is financially worse off than if she had stayed home. In fact, this is the situation for many families even when not paying child care, because the family has the illusion that it is financially better off now that the wife is earning a paycheck. Dr. Mason notes that such families often get into financial trouble buying items on credit that they could not previously afford because they have erroneously assumed that they have $10,000 to spend when they actually have less than $2,000. Since in many cases the wife's actual contribution to the family income is insignificant, the budget becomes even less flexible as it stretches to cover these additional installment payments.

What is perhaps more tragic is that many women enter lower-paying jobs than Mary's and in many cases have little or nothing to show for their forty hours of weekly employment. This is especially tragic for those who did not want to work outside the home in the first place. This brings us to the point that family security is often traded for minimal financial gain. Furthermore, families with employed wives save less than other families with the same total income.

Miracles Can Happen When a Family Pulls Together

Other families are left in worse circumstances than Mary's. One such family was left by the father when the youngest child was four months old. "It was a traumatic time with a difficult divorce, but the courageous mother was full of faith and determined that she would do everything she could to succeed as a single parent. . . .

"This mother gathered her children about her and explained their situation. There were back payments due on the house, current bills of every sort, and no income. They could turn to others for help, but if they were willing to work together as a family, she thought they could keep their house and make it, once more, a happy home. They were willing. Every child who was old enough found a way to help earn some money. They cut lawns, delivered papers, tended babies, collected aluminum cans, did housework. One of the older children took the responsibility for the gas bill, another for the lights; the mother put her earnings toward the house payments. They limited other spending to bare necessities.

"In time, the house payments were caught up; they were able to meet their other obligations and actually invest in some small, inexpensive properties they could fix up to generate income. This enabled the mother to be at home."[12]

Can the mother at home have financial security? Yes, she can. There are exceptions to every rule, but if a woman desires to be in the home, she can, with financial planning, careful budgeting, and creative thinking!

MYTH 7

When Dad Won't Help, Mom Is Helpless

We see mothers throw their arms up in despair when facing too much work and stress. We see mothers drowning in depression. We even see mothers walk out, completely giving up on the family and marriage. Even the most competent mother at home can't be everything. She simply can't do it all. The mother of the last century felt the crunch, as the old verse reveals:

A man's work ends from dusk to dawn,
But a woman's work is *never* done.

If a husband can't or won't help with homemaking, this is a serious blow to the wife's workload. Furthermore, his refusal to help psychologically weakens and mars the status of the work. Implied in such a refusal is the belief that the work is degrading and beneath the dignity of a man. It is thus important that the psychological implications be addressed, understood, and changed.

When her husband doesn't help, a wife tends to feel there's nothing she can do. With these feelings, it is easy to understand the despair and resentment of the overworked wife. She suffers unfairly; she has no support system. But is this myth only a myth? When her husband won't help, is there nothing the wife can do?

Challenging the Myth

Actually, most husbands help, and some *are* helping more these days. There is evidence that attitudes toward working in the home and helping women are changing among the younger generation of men. In one study of blue-collar husbands in Madison, Wisconsin, it was found that the average male was doing up to about 30 percent of the child care in the family where the average age of the children was still in the preschool years. They tended to agree with the statement that they would do even more child rearing if their jobs weren't so constraining.[1] Admittedly, this study reports a higher percentage of husband help than most, but it does signify a change. One interesting note is that husbands whose wives are employed don't help much more than husbands whose wives remain home.

Ron is one example of this more modern trend of husbands helping more. Ron, a college athlete, was a senior when he started dating his future wife. They were married shortly after his graduation. Ron received a commission in the Air Force and was absent two or three days each week on missile alert for the first four years of their marriage. His wife worked full-time at a school near the Air Force Base, and on days that she worked he was off duty. She would come home to a full-course dinner and a clean house. Ron scrubbed floors, cleaned windows, washed laundry, and so on. He enjoyed cooking and would even bake cookies. When he got home after a day on alert he would also be greeted by a warm dinner and a clean house. During the years that they both worked, they had a fifty-fifty partnership in caring for the home. As the children arrived and Ron's wife quit her job to be with them, Ron still offered help and support in the home. He found enjoyment in his children. He gave his new son his first bath, changed and washed diapers, and took turns with the night feedings. He encouraged his wife to pursue her personal interests along with being a wife and mother. He provided a babysitter one day each week so she could shop, go to the spa, take a class, or learn a hobby.

There were periods in Ron's marriage when his wife took over all home responsibilities, such as when he was working full-time and also going to school for an advanced degree. There have also been times when Ron took over more home responsibilities, such as when his wife was working toward a degree. Women should know that there are men who are helping—and their marriages thrive. Such exemplary men can provide hope and direction for many couples.

Trends among Men, Women, and Work in the Home

Three thousand high school seniors in a 1982 national survey gave their opinions about family and work in their prospective marriages.[2] Responses from these young people indicate that in the future there will be mothers in the home, but also more fathers helping.

For couples without children, the seniors thought that men should work full-time and women part-time. For couples with children, their most common preference was for men to work full-time and women not to work. Most disapprove of a husband who would not work when his wife was employed and supporting them well. The students hold the husband accountable for the economic support of the family even if his wife is successfully employed.

In the area of division of child care, they feel that even if a man is the only one employed, he should have equal responsibility for child care during the hours when both parents are at home. A dad shouldn't be relieved of child care just because he's the sole breadwinner. If both parents are employed, evenings and weekends should be shared equally. Although most seniors felt there should be an equal sharing role for the care of children, many felt it acceptable if the responsibility rested ultimately on the woman.

In the area of division of housework, they felt housework should be shared equally between partners if both are working—females favor this stronger than males. But although these high school seniors believe there should be equal sharing of duties between marital partners, they still see the final responsibility as resting with the partner who has traditionally held the particular duty.

Newly Marrieds' Division of Labor

In a 1984 study involving 120 couples who had been married from one to three months, researchers asked who did what tasks over a two- to three-week period. Women did 4.4 tasks per day (4.1 feminine tasks and 0.3 masculine tasks) and men did 2.2 tasks per day (1.4 feminine and 0.8 masculine). It should be pointed out here that husbands worked outside the home an average of 40.6 hours per week and wives averaged 28.2 hours per week. In analyzing all this data, the researchers found that the more hours the husband was employed in comparison to the wife, the less housework he did, and that division of labor in and out of the home followed a more traditional pattern for men who worked more. They still found that women did most of the housework regardless of their outside employment.[3]

Middle-Class Couples' Divisions of Labor

In a similar study of 164 parents, published in 1985, the goal was to determine whether or not greater role sharing was indeed taking place, as compared to earlier studies. The couples in this study had been married for an average of twelve years. The study showed that there seemed to be more egalitarianism regarding child care and decision making, but the wife still did most household jobs. However, men who were high in "expressiveness" (that is, being kind and sensitive to others) helped their wives more.

Moreover, the more expressive the wife was, the more help she received. Additionally, men who were aggressive, dominant, and "tough" helped less in the home and shared less decision making with the wives.[4] It appears that personality influences participation in household work.

One researcher said that gender role attitudes are "becoming more liberal," but it's happening slowly. In this study 10 to 40 percent of those interviewed believed that "men should do more housework and child care." He found that married working women are spending 39 hours on their jobs plus 25 hours per week in housework, for a total of 64 work hours. Married men had 48.5 hours on their jobs and 12.6 hours per week in home tasks, to total 61 work hours.[5] Again, there is evidence for a trend toward more male participation in the home.

If Your Husband Is Not Helping, Why?

There are various reasons why a husband may not be helping as much as a wife would like. Here are some questions to consider:

1. Does he view housework as strictly a female's responsibility—a threat to his masculine stereotype?
2. Is he concerned that his help will interfere with his job as breadwinner?
3. Does he know what you would like him to do?
4. Do you support and appreciate his efforts in the home?
5. Does he feel he has no time to put into the home?
6. Does he see the value of helping in the home?

The Masculine Stereotype Problem

If a husband views housework as strictly a female responsibility, he has likely come from a family in which his father has not helped. If your husband has not seen his father washing dishes and mopping floors, these activities might pose a threat to his masculine image. Some men are insecure about their male self-image and need to defend their supposed position of authority. One way for them to keep their "upper position" is to put women down and to categorize homemaking and even child care as women's work.

But most men in this category are simply following the role models set for them. The most visible men in our society are those on TV, and judging by men's program selection, the role models they see would mostly be football players, commentators, politicians, or criminals. If a man looks around his world and sees only these men, who never work inside the home, he naturally is going to assume that this is the life of real men. Even if a sizeable percentage of other men were involved with child care, your husband would rarely see them.

The men he should be seeing are less visible: men who are home with their wives and children. These men must become more visible. As they become more public, this cultural masculine stereotype will change. What can be done? The key is to help husbands become aware of the many other men who do give a fair hand to their wives. Visit their homes and ask who does what. Your husband may be surprised!

The Traditional Breadwinner Problem

Along with the male image just discussed is another reason men do not help in the home: they perceive housework as interfering with their role as breadwinner outside the home. For centuries, the man has been the breadwinner. As would be expected, even today his profession or job is extremely important to him. His job, his success, defines his manhood. Many men stay in the same job until retirement. Even those who change jobs typically stay with the same job for long segments of their life, and all but 10 percent stay employed until they retire. So men may feel that if they are able to bring home the bacon, what more should anyone ask? Thus, their role as breadwinner may be competing with their role in the home as husband and father.

According to Arlene Cardozo, more families are realizing that a man's work can be better integrated with family life. She tells us that in the years to come many more men are likely to integrate their jobs with their home life so that they can enjoy both, without as much pressure from either. This kind of integration is especially effective for families with fathers in service professions such as medicine, clergical, or "people-centered work." (Also, we'd like to add that home computers have brought, and will bring, many men home.) Cardozo goes on to say, "If a man is committed to both a people-centered home and people-centered work, integrating these two elements of his life into a cohesive whole is more effective than trying to separate them, since people never seem to get sick, or to have personal emergencies, between nine and five. Also, living near work serves the needs of many men who are fed up with commuting. These men prefer a more relaxed kind of back-and-forth between home and office; in some cases they office right in their homes." She points out the advantages to those families who can view living and working as part of a whole way of life. They integrate the two spheres of living as much as possible.[6]

Deborah Fallows gives an excellent example of how her husband works from an office in their home. "He gets several dozen telephone calls each day, often at dinnertime; collects mounds of junk mail, and meets visitors. But it also means that he is home, near the family, most of the time. Jim can usually arrange his working hours with some flexibility. That means he can see the boys in the morning when they get up; he sometimes drives them to school; when they are home for lunch, he can eat with them. He regularly sees them when they get home from school." She tells us that they almost always have the evenings together, for dinner and the bedtime routine of bath, books, and bed. These advantages come at a considerable cost to her husband's working life. She has heard him turn down breakfast, dinner, and evening meetings to be with his sons, and he'll work late at night to make up for daytime interludes he has spent with his children. Because many of his friends and colleagues are single or childless, he sees them sit down for an afternoon of uninterrupted work on a Saturday or Sunday. Realizing this, Deborah says, "I can tell he's thinking how much more quickly he could finish an article or book if he were similarly unencumbered. In short, he's made a trade: ambitious as he is, he has accepted less success—and money—than he might otherwise have. In exchange he has gotten to know his sons."[7]

A Man's Role in the Home

Sometimes a husband does not know what to do in the home. Maybe there is a communication gap between husband and wife. Possibly she expects him to take care of certain things although she has never discussed her needs with him. This would lead to continued frustration and disappointment.

In the past, society has not assigned men a strong role in the home. The husband took care of the yard and garage, while the wife did the rest. So our man rolls up the garden hose, sweeps walks, shovels snow, cleans garages, and even washes the outside of windows. Notice that everything a man has traditionally done is located outside—outside the home! Men have been motivated to put their labor and their minds on things other than in the home.

A husband may be willing to help more in the home but doesn't because: (1) he hasn't thought of it on his own, or (2) he doesn't know what to do.

One friend mentioned that her husband likes her to delegate to him chores and repairs in the home. He enjoys having a Saturday chore list—his list of "Honey-do's." Other husbands may want to delegate and make assignments.

Some husbands are extremely sensitive about being approached to do household chores. In such cases it certainly would be advisable not to demean or criticize. Begin by discarding hidden resentments that may be nagging at you. Decide when would be the best time to bring the issue into open discussion. Tell him directly you simply cannot do it all. You might outline specifically what needs to be done. The following example illustrates how one young woman handled the problem.

"Even though I have only been married for two months, I have found that letting my husband choose what jobs he wants to do in the house or giving him the jobs that are more fun enables me to have his help more often. At first we almost instinctively fell into the popular man/woman roles with jobs in the home. I did mostly everything to do with the cleaning and Dennis took out the garbage and did the repair jobs. That got old really quick and I found I needed his help as well. So when a movie came that we wanted to see or on the weekends, we'd try to clean the house before we left. I let Dennis choose what he wanted to do or if he didn't care, I'd give him the front room or bedroom to clean (the less discouraging jobs) while I cleaned the bathroom and the kitchen. The work went quickly and it was such a nice feeling of satisfaction for both of us and we could go to our desired activity much quicker."

Appreciating Efforts in the Home Problem

It would be difficult for husbands to enjoy helping in the home if their efforts were not appreciated. One young woman said, "My mother has never encouraged my father to work inside with her. Instead, she sends him outside to do yard work to get him out of her way."

One friend would restack the dishes in the dishwasher after her husband had filled it. "Why bother?" he said finally. "She'll just do it over anyway!"

New parents may struggle with this concept at the arrival of a baby. The mother may feel that only she knows how to change or bathe their infant. Fortunately, most new mothers want and encourage dads to be involved.

Deborah Fallows wrote about her feelings of appreciation for the help of her husband: "[It] has meant a great deal to me. . . . It has meant that Jim knows what I have done as a mother all day long. He has seen me cry on a perfectly normal morning and recognizes it comes from fatigue, exasperation, and general state that's part of caring for a three-year-old preschooler and a three-month-old infant. He has seen the efforts I've put in at this job of mothering, from the physical demands of lugging babies, groceries, strollers, to the emotional demands of keeping company with small children for ten hours at a time. He has seen me worry about how, amid all this, I am to find time to be a person myself too. He has responded in ways that he could. When the boys were little, it meant he could cock an ear to their bedroom doors while they were napping and I could run off to do a necessary errand. It meant he understood that I needed some time by myself and would offer, before I had to ask for it, a regular respite on Saturday morning or an impromptu evening during the week. It meant he encouraged me to get help with cleaning or a few hours of babysitting, even though they took what seemed like a disproportionate chunk of our budget. Most of all, he displays respect for the work that I am doing in raising the boys. He considers it, in the larger scheme of things, to be more important than his own work, or any other work."[8]

Putting Time into the Home Problem

Often a husband feels that he has no time for the home, that if he must help with child care and housework, it will take time from another activity. Wives usually appreciate having husbands as breadwinners, so unless a man is a "workaholic," time taken for his work is a legitimate reason for not being home to help.

But it is the after-work hours we are addressing. Some men return home to watch TV or read the paper while the wife is preparing dinner and struggling with children underfoot. Other men head for the golf course, health club, or gym. Often when a man is unknowingly negligent in his time with home and family, it is because the wife has not communicated her needs to him. Janet says: "When my first son was born I spent months trying to adjust to my new schedule and find some time for *me*! Finally, one morning as my husband left for work, I blurted in frustration, 'You spend five hours a week playing basketball, but I have not one hour to write.' He looked at me, half-astonished that he hadn't realized I had *no* free time, and defensively stated, 'I will give you as much time in the library as I take to play basketball!' I took him up on it, and for months went to the library every Saturday morning."

One possible solution would be to agree that the hours from eight to five comprise the husband's time at the office and the wife's time to care for the family. After the "eight-to-five" day, the partners go on a role-sharing system. Realizing and communicating expectations to each other creates a more efficient and united family. Ask yourself what kind of help you want from your husband. Then communicate your feelings. Each woman's needs will be different.

One wife wanted her husband to be with their son as much as possible when he was home. They found several ways to do this, such as having him sit by their son at meals, bathe him each night, get him ready for bed, and read a bedtime story. They also realized the need to build pleasant moments between him and his son, such as wrestling, going for walks, talking, father-son interviews, and swinging—times for just the two of them to enjoy one another.

The Value of the Husband's Help in the Home

There are some reasons why husbands may actually want to help. Perhaps you could point out that if he helped it would give you and him more time together, both during the housework period and after. One practical couple, both students, has learned to share household chores. She writes: "On a typical Saturday morning, my husband goes to the Laundromat while I stay home and bathe the baby, wash dishes, vacuum, dust, and take care of other household chores. If there is something I cannot get done while he is doing the laundry, then my husband helps me with it when he gets home. Then, after all the housework is done, we do something fun such as go to a movie, go swimming, go out to eat, or just go for a ride."

Another student remembers her father mopping floors or vacuuming while her mother dusted or cooked. One day, in her late teens, after being unimpressed by the "macho" boys she was meeting, she asked her mother how she got her father to help in the home. The answer came as quite a surprise to a sixteen-year-old. The mother said, "I didn't. In fact he never helped around the house when we were first married. At first it never really bothered me, either. But when I had three little children, it began to get difficult. Your father was gone so much because we were in the Air Force and I wanted to be sure we didn't drift apart, because I spent my daily hours doing different things than he did. So when he *was* home, I would say to him, 'Gerald, come talk to me while I do the dishes, or laundry, or dusting, or whatever.' I would listen to your dad's description of his days and his duties while I worked on housework and my children were either outside or taking naps. Pretty soon, your father would unconsciously join in with the work while he talked to me, and over the years we've learned to enjoy doing the housework together because it gave us our time to talk to each other."

When a husband helps in the home, he is setting an example of mutually working together, showing to the children their mother and father cooperating, setting a role model for his sons, and giving the family more contact with their father. Simply stated, a husband needs to know that when he helps in the home, it gives him a stronger role as the father, as well as the husband.

A man needs to be aware that long-term happiness is family based. The genuine and most basic strokes, the rewards of life, will come from those close personal relationships he forms with his wife and children, rather than his very good relationships with his colleagues at work or his companions in recreation.

Has anyone heard of a man's deathbed statement being, "I wish I had spent more time with the business"? Neither will you find his boss, or his golf and fishing buddies, at his deathbed! It's interesting to note how many men have spent their lives working toward retirement and reached that goal with one regret: that they didn't spend more time with their families.

MYTH 8

There Is No Reward in Housework

Many researchers have tried to place a dollar value on housework. An average of four of the most recent of these figures is $10,138, based on the hourly wage you would have to pay someone to do the housework alone.[1]

It is unfortunate—"maddening" would be more accurate—that our society bases respect for work on the amount of money it brings. Because visible money is not produced by doing housework, many sneer, believing it is without worth. They overlook what the authors of a family textbook show is a most important contribution: "enriching the quality of life."[2]

This current myth that devalues housework—where did it originate? Kathleen Slaugh Bahr, a family life specialist, says housework once held a favored position in society because goods were produced in the home. In this setting, anything done for the home directly benefited production and was highly valued.[3]

When industrialization came, women in the nineteenth century took their productive tasks from the home and performed them in factories. Women then were able to show a dollar value for their work. A monster was being born. Women began to devalue housework. The juxtaposition of money against housework has wrought a negative effect on our society by robbing women of one of their prime sources of value. According to Rae André, it is accurate to say that child care, family maintenance, and home management have progressively declined in status to the point that they are viewed as only necessary and insignificant labor.[4] We don't need the weekly Sunday supplement to tell us that family relationships and traditional values have been declining as the emergence of women in the work force has been increasing. As women do more outside the home, it is often concluded that they are escaping. But let's examine how an average woman today really feels about housework. Is there really no reward in it?

Challenging the Myth

According to the U.S. Bureau of Labor Statistics for 1982, less than 11 percent of employed women were in professional and managerial jobs; most were in clerical, service, sales, and blue-collar jobs.[5] An examination of these jobs will show that most women are highly supervised, do not have flexible schedules, and do not have creative work with self-directing opportunities. Housework compares quite favorably with those jobs on the scale of being self-directing.

For the many women who find housework a joy rather than a drudgery, there is a basic difference in their perception of what housework means. These women can see beyond the cleaning process. For example, Dorothy Lund, in her article, "Pardon Me, but I LIKE Housework," has this to say:

> If we do not make our bed every morning, it should not be a matter calling for 20 lashes. Each day has its demands. But if you want to make a bed tenderly, begin with fresh bottom linen pulled crisp and taut. Next comes a top sheet floating lightly as a lily on a pond. Then a warm, airy covering is tucked gently over the bed, with some give at the corners. Climbing into

such a bed restores the soul and eases the body into sleep. . . .

Ironing is the most contemplative of domestic chores. It allows the mind to skim over the wrinkled surface of tempting ideas or knotty problems, seeking a smooth solution. I have often worked my way through a mountain of laundry and been greatly surprised to get to the bottom of my current dilemma as I reached the bottom of the basket. It's no accident that nations speak of "ironing out" difficulties.

Cooking, on the other hand, is a more complex skill. Even a simple meal requires full attention. I dare not cook while arguing, rejoicing, or puzzling over a real family crisis, since I may scorch the beans or put in too much salt.

The cook is similar to the painter. When I was a child I got a box of paints every Christmas. Now as I chop up black olives, radishes, or fresh green scallions to give a splash of color to an otherwise dull-looking dish, I'm reminded of the pleasure I used to get dipping my brush into those new colors. And cooking is perhaps the only kind of housework where the crowd may cheer and call for encores.

If spring cleaning threatens to overwhelm me, I think, "Windows!" Washing windows may be the quickest thrill around. A few sprays of window cleaner, a few swipes with paper towel or newspaper, and suddenly I've got a crystal-clear view of the back-yard birdbath. Watching the splashdown of feathered visitors renews me. And when I hear a bird crying proudly, "My nest! My nest!" I'm moved to put my own nest in order.

There is something mindlessly soothing about polishing well-loved pieces of furniture. It puts a balm on small irritations as well as on the tabletops.

It takes blood, sweat and tears to keep copper, brass and silver bright and shining. I tackle pans and irons while waiting up for children. I go after silver when someone's sick. Polishing has often helped me make it through a difficult day. And during the long, dead

> time after real tragedy, such daily housework builds a bridge between despair and living again.[6]

Doris Lund's perception of her housework is not exceptional. There are many women in every community who have similar feelings about their work in the home. These women take pride in their homemaking and housekeeping skills, seeing their contributions as having *intrinsic* value.

There are a few who may become too compulsive about cleaning, sacrificing family relationships for the sake of a clean home. Housework then becomes a resented drudgery by family members, and we are better off to hire help or even forgo some chores, where possible. But if used correctly, housework can be a vehicle for family unity, task competence, and self-development in family members.

One mother of eight and homemaker-author, Daryl Hoole, wisely says, "An ideal home is like an apprentice shop where children learn skills, habits, responsibility, dependability, and self-discipline. It is especially important that children are trained to develop self-discipline. It's not difficult to learn to make a bed; the challenge lies in making it *every* day! And children who gain mastery over little things (such as making beds) will have power over greater things."[7]

Family Relationships and Unity

For Professor Kathleen Slaugh Bahr, there is much more to housework than clean windows, shiny floors, or even nutritious meals. The greatest benefit, says Bahr, lies in the development of human relations. Work has long been recognized as an avenue for self-development. And housework gives an opportunity for parents and children to work together—and communicate.

The rewards of working together cannot be underestimated. Where does a child begin relating to other individuals? In the home. And housework provides excellent opportunities. In this perspective, housework is not seen as a negative experience, but rather as a chance to be with another person who is important to you, to talk to that person about things other than the work you're doing, and to model positive social skills. For example, instead of pushing Billy or Susi, kicking and screaming, to the laundry room to fold clothes, a parent has the opportunity to say, "We can talk while we fold these clothes," or "Let's talk about *allowances* while we fold some clothes." This time together is not for prying but for honest, open disclosure about areas that you share in common, about what you're doing through the day and week, about funny things you notice, philosophies of life, new jokes, and so on. Being with another person in a work context is valuable and develops closeness.

Even the most mundane tasks can be channeled into priceless moments together, as Janet learned one morning when she had a lot to do. In her words: "It seemed as if my little boys, Bridger and Kendal, ages three and two respectively, could not get enough of my attention. Finally, in a desperate attempt to involve them and get *one* thing accomplished before noon, I gave them each a plastic bag to 'help' me do the laundry. We went to each hamper, collecting the colored clothes in one bag and the whites in another. The boys thought this was great and it showed them there is a little skill involved in separating laundry.

"When that was done, I told Bridger, 'Take Kendal and go on down and put these in the washer.' He was delighted! He went ahead of me and by the time I got there he had dutifully put the clothes in what he thought was the washer—except it was the dryer. Surprised that my three-year-old didn't know the difference, I showed him which one was the washer and talked to him about how the water comes into the house from pipes under the street. I told him how the water comes into the washer and set both boys up to watch the washer fill. They were really amazed and interested! Then I let them put the soap in. They had a great time and learned a few things (and I got the laundry done)." Although it takes more effort, this experience reminds us once again how children need involvement.

When it is time for yard work, parents can build a great deal of family cohesion by planning and structuring it as a positive, social experience. Everyone benefits by working together: you get the work done; they learn to work. Small children can learn about plants and weeds, seasons, annuals, perennials, evergreen and deciduous trees, and why leaves change colors with the seasons.

Task Competence

Most of us have witnessed the tragedy and lost potential in a person who has not learned to work. These people are not happy, competent, or adequate. Following through on a daily task cannot be underestimated as a way of developing individual competence. This is a leadership and teaching responsibility that falls heavily on the mother.

Children are much too smart these days to buy into "Do as I say, not as I do." Thus, a mother must first be a good example. We cannot justly expect our children to do their daily tasks without modeling the way we do our own daily tasks. In addition, task competence is the foundation in building basic adequacy and self-esteem. Structuring jobs that you can do with the children, and assigning jobs according to ability, are vehicles for helping them be better people.

Completing tasks is also an important way to build confidence. Gayle says: "Robert is by far the most messy of the six. (Perhaps I've forgotten how messy a two-year-old can be.) Although he's a darling, he can take a meal of banana and cereal and redecorate the kitchen. He did it again this morning. As I *patiently* got him down from his stool and cleaned him off, I said, 'Did you make this mess?' He said, 'Yeah.' I said, 'Don't make messes if you're not going to clean them up.'

"Then I said, 'Here's something you can help me do. Take this empty wastebasket to Daddy's desk.' He was so excited to help. He kept saying, 'I did it! I did it!' all the way up the stairs."

A mother often finds that getting a child to complete a task is more difficult than doing it herself. One mother of seven opted to implement a token economy as incentive for her children who were in some bad habits of nonperformance, evoking continual nagging. The change was striking! Here's how it worked:

Each child's name was listed on a chart. Mother and children together listed all the things they could think of that needed to be done and usually required reminding. These included brushing teeth, putting away clothes, doing homework before eight o'clock, clearing the table, folding laundry, washing a floor or window, sweeping the porch, washing the car, getting to school on time, getting in bed on time, saying something kind, or being a peacemaker in a problem.

Each task was worth at least one point on the chart. After a child accumulated five points he or she received a star. Each star was worth a small monetary amount. (In this case it was worth twenty cents.) A bonus point was awarded if Mother didn't have to remind them. Soon beds were made before school, counters and mirrors were free from spots, even the lights were turned off instead of being left on! With no nagging! Mother began to feel that the small amount of money she would be paying out was worth the emotional drain of reminding. But she comically confided, "I really don't mind picking up a pair of socks now because I know it's a savings for myself!" But completing the chore was not as important as training the child.

The Joy of Giving

No monetary value can ever be placed on the sense of value that comes through service. This feeling cannot be purchased. A great example of this idea is put forth in the following excerpt from anthropologist Dorothy Lee, who discovered the value of working in the home:

It was Christmas Eve; I was working late at night, listening to the desultory talk of my husband and my brother-in-law. I was exhausted after a day of housework, of coping with two small children, of Christmas preparations; but I had to finish making bedding for a doll crib, and I was working against time, wishing I were in bed.

I had been living a life of conflict since my marriage, since I had felt that I owed it to my profession to continue my work in anthropology. This meant that I had to organize my life so that my housewifely duties did not encroach unduly on my professional work; and I had to justify everything that I did as a housewife, as something imposed by the exigencies of my budget or my role as wife and mother. In this way, I did not have to feel guilty toward my profession. The doll blanket I was making that night was amply justified; it would give happiness to my three-year-old daughter, and it had been necessary for me to take the time to make crib and bedding, for I could not afford to buy them.

As I sewed this Christmas Eve, I was suddenly astonished to discover that I had started to add an entirely unpremeditated and unnecessary edging of embroidery; and, simultaneously, I was aware of a deep enjoyment in what I was doing. It was a feeling that had nothing to do with the pleasure the work would give to my daughter on the morrow; it had nothing to do with a sense of achievement, or of virtue in duty accomplished. And I knew that I had never liked to embroider. There was no justification for my work; yet it was the source of such a deep satisfaction, that the late hour and my fatigue had ceased to exist for me.

At this moment of discovery, I knew that I was experiencing what it meant to be a social being, not merely Dorothy Lee, an individual; I knew that I had truly become a mother, a wife, a neighbor, a teacher. I realized that some boundary had disappeared, so that I was working in a social medium; that I was not working for the future pleasure of a distant daughter, but

> rather within a relationship unaffected by temporality or physical absence. What gave meaning to my work was the medium in which I was working—the medium of love, in a broad sense. So far, my rationalization and justification of my work had obscured this meaning, had cut me off from my own social context. It suddenly became clear to me that it did not matter whether I was scrubbing the kitchen floor or darning stockings or zipping up snowsuits; these all had meaning, not in themselves, but in terms of the situation of which they were a part. They contained social value because they implemented the value of the social situation.[8]

Dorothy Lee goes on to compare this feeling with the work she had done with the Tikopia society. She came to realize that this was the way they worked together socially, and she finally understood what motivated them. She was no longer puzzled about why father, mother, aunt, and grandmother all worked together firing the oven, grating coconut, nursing babies. Children ran errands, forming a bridge between the young and the old. Jokes and anecdotes flew back and forth. No one wanted to be alone, and work was the cement that bound the families together.

"We Shape Our Houses, Then Our Houses Shape Us"

Is there no reward in housework? Does it not occur to the critics that we may find fulfillment in cleaning and beautifying our homes, as Doris Lund described? Just as a farmer can love the work on his land, a homemaker can love the toil of her labors in the home. As Winston Churchill said, "We shape our houses, then our houses shape us."

We gain further insight into the value of homemaking from a mother who describes the growth that comes from tedious chores: "As mothers, our work is not washing diapers and mending holes in jeans—that is what we spend much of our time doing, but it is not our work. Our work is rearing children to be successful, to fulfill their potential. . . . Jeans may have to be mended and dishes washed, gardens tended, floors swept, and beds made, but all these things are gifts of God to us. They are tools that we may use to develop . . . and help our children develop. We sweep floors, weed gardens, tend babies, and learn and grow—our spirits along with our bodies."

Another mother tells a story of her small son who elevated household chores to a position of notable quality: "It had been one of my usual busy days—housework, cleaning and caring for the children—jobs that I would repeat the next day and the next. But it had been an exciting day for my five-year-old son. A group of youngsters from our church had been taken to visit some shut-ins. Johnny came home bubbling with talk of the trip and the sick ladies. I put Johnny to bed a little earlier that evening, and as is our bedtime custom, I listened to his prayers. This night his prayer was different. 'And please, God,' he added, 'please help those ladies get well so they can hang out clothes and wash dishes like Mommie.' I stood there in the darkened room, looking down at Johnny's sleepy head on the pillow. It was a moment of quiet revelation. I felt humble—the very best that my son could hope for someone else was a life just like mine. Suddenly the morning's dirty dishes and unmade beds became my blessings."[9]

Janet's five-year-old son often expresses his feelings to his mother about how wonderful her role is. In fact, she once overheard a conversation between her sons, Bridger, five, and Kendal, three. "Kendal, don't you want to be the daddy?" asked Bridger, "because the daddy is the strongest person in the family."

Janet thought that Bridger was finally learning the importance of the father's role as she stepped in the room and asked, "What are you boys doing?"

"Well," explained Bridger, "Kendal wants to be the mama, and I want to be the mama. Someone has to be the daddy so I'm trying to get Kendal to!"

Our perception of our work in the home is the key to how rewarding it will be to us.

MYTH 9

Homemaking Is a Dead-end Role

We had an interesting conversation with a talented mother-at-home who has published, written, and editorialized to the stay-at-home mom.

"You might have a difficult time getting your book published," she warned.

"Because we have no track record?"

"Well, partly. But another problem will be that publishers tend to think mothers at home are illiterate—that their only interests are watching the neighbors next door and soap operas."

"Really?" We agonized, thinking this all the more reason for our book—to combat this ignorant image that has far too long been attached to our role!

Prejudice Against Mothers at Home

The March 31, 1986, edition of *Newsweek* tells us that the majority of both the working and nonworking mothers surveyed said they thought it had become less socially acceptable for mothers to stay home full-time to raise their children. " 'Right now there is real prejudice against women who don't work,' says Marjorie Hansen-Shaevitz, a La Jolla,

Calif., psychologist who has studied women's changing roles. Women at home, she says, often feel like failures. 'They can't be only a perfect mother, wife and homemaker,' she says. 'They have to be a perfect worker too.' Rachel Grigsby, 30, a Los Angeles mother who stayed home until her oldest child was in first grade, remembers the prejudice. 'People would come up to you at parties,' she says, 'and ask, "What else do you do besides being a mother?" I'd get real mad and tell them it's hard work. But by that time they were moving off to find somebody more interesting.' "[1]

A couple of years ago, a respected man in our community suggested to Janet, "You have too much going to spend your life with your head in a diaper pail!" The belittling of our creative work to the drudgeries of diaper-pail existence is a little hard to stomach. Today's feminists, in their zeal to create alternative life-styles for women, have often neglected to portray a positive image of the mother at home. Linda Burton, career woman and one of the founders of "Mothers at Home," says, "We have fostered a generation of young people who have heard nothing but put-downs about child-rearing. . . . They have been encouraged to 'do something' more important with their lives. They [mothers at home] are considered intellectually inferior and out of pace with the times."[2]

Mothers at Home Have Multiple Roles

Most mothers at home have experienced society's ostracism, but who do we "believe" we are—really? As a young, single mother of the seventies, Janet struggled on a poverty level to remain home with her three preschoolers. Eventually she found herself filling out a government form, hoping for assistance. "I remember the heading 'occupation.' Should I leave it blank or fill it in? I debated and then quickly scrawled 'homemaker.' The receptionist glanced over it and snickered aloud, 'Homemaker?' I can't remember my verbal response, but will never forget the feeling of humiliation. It was difficult enough to decide to be there; but to be placed on the defensive with my one strong identity was more than I could bear. I vaguely remember hiding trickles of tears with a bent head as I cared for my little ones, clamoring around me."

What are we—mothers at home—homemakers—full-time mothers? Actually most of us are, in part, hygienist, economist, beautician, care giver, philosopher, teacher, counselor, nutritionist, custodian, cook, gardener, interior decorator, nurse, plumber, and the list goes on. Oh yes, and we must be a little bit "comedian," for after that list, who could survive without a sense of humor?

As Shakespeare said, "What's in a name? A rose by any other name would smell as sweet." Not in all cases! We think the term *housewife* must be done away with; it indicates that the wife is married to house rather than spouse. And *housekeeper* implies that housework is the crux of our responsibility at home, rather than child care. The most current terms for our role are *home manager* and *domestic engineer*, but they sound so businesslike. We choose the term *homemaker*: one who creates a home—the resting place from the world's cares, our hearth for nurturing loved ones.

The Myth That Money, Power, and Recognition Make Women Happy

Saren is a typical example of a woman who truly believed she would be unhappy in the home. And so she never stayed there. Instead, she sought exotic adventures, travel, and the glamors of life.

Saren did marry right after high school graduation, but had no children, and divorced a few years later. Today Saren is a brilliant and talented fashion designer, lives in a spacious beach house, drives a new sports car, and must be the envy of other women. But now that she is nearing middle age, she is beginning to question her life-style. She feels that something is missing. She calls her homemaker friends on the telephone and ruminates on their different lives, the different directions each has chosen. She confides to her friends how fortunate they are to have beautiful families. She wonders if it is too late for her to change course so that she may somehow find greater fulfillment in life.

America has always valued self-development and emphasized individualism. Yet there is a dangerous paradox in the focus on self-fulfillment, for such a focus can lead to self-indulgence.

Psychologists are now beginning to acknowledge an error in their early formulations that supposed a focus on the self was the way to self-development. Could it be that focusing on others is a better way to achieve personal growth? Michael A. Wallach, professor of psychology, and Lise Wallach, lecturer in psychology, both at Duke University, tell us in their book *Psychology's Sanction for Selfishness*: "The psychological emphasis on fulfillment and freedom . . . may be counter to much of what helps to give people a sense of meaning in their lives. Meaning may depend to a large degree on assuming and carrying out responsibilities for one another. Having social purposes beyond ourselves may be relevant to our mental health, with contributions to meeting the needs of others a source of our own satisfaction."[3]

One of the foremost sociologists of our time, Urie Bronfenbrenner, has spoken out about the alarming long-term problems incurred in a society which emphasizes seeking rewards primarily for oneself: "America has temporarily lost its balance. Today, what matters most for many people is their own growth and happiness, their own self-fulfillment. We seem to be sunk in individualism. We want so much to 'make it' for ourselves that we have almost stopped being a caring society that cares for others. We seem to be hesitant about making a commitment to anyone or anything, including our own flesh and blood."

He points out that individualism has helped bring about extraordinary efforts by Americans. But he believes we now need to put other, neglected values on the scale. He feels we have many other traditions in the American past and we should draw on them also. It's a matter of more balanced attitudes. He concludes: "The healthy growth of each child requires a commitment of love, care, and attention from someone. Neighbors, day-care leaders, and school teachers can help; but most of the enduring, irrational involvement and intimate activities must come from parents. No one else can care so much or so continually. We need to get out of ourselves and into the lives of our children more than we do."[4]

Dr. Bronfenbrenner realizes that as the Sarens of the world (and their male counterparts) go traipsing off to "fulfill themselves and their great destinies," the children are the first ones who suffer, but the adults will follow.

Where Does True Success Lie?

Saren's power, fame, and wealth are typical results of America's search for individualism. We have always been a "Horatio Alger" country, praising those few who have come from nothing to obtain acclaim through hard work, sacrifice, and perseverance. The great inventors, financiers, statesmen, artists, authors, and movie stars are those to whom we give our attention and affection. But we fail to notice that so many of these achievers, though abounding in power, money, and material rewards, are unsuccessful in achieving true happiness. Many of them commit suicide, drug themselves into oblivion, suffer with poor marriages, and leave a legacy of self-indulgence.

There is another group of high achievers whom we might examine. Psychologists Abraham Maslow and Carl Rogers discovered the qualities of character that contribute to balanced success. The theories of these two psychologists have been criticized for much of modern psychology's focus on the self; even Wallach and Wallach, for example, have blamed them. But a careful study of these theories reveals that they really recommend achieving a "better self" by self-sacrifice, delayed gratification, and thinking of others as much as oneself. Their philosophies have often been misinterpreted and misused.

For example, some characteristics of Maslow's "self-actualized" person are described in the box on pages 94-95, with a companion statement showing how to look outside the self.

The characteristics described by Maslow are desirable for every person but achieved by only a few. They are characteristics possessed by productive people he identified in history and in his own social world. And yet these people were not bound by social status, affluence, or money. They were not bound by sex, race, or even handicaps. After studying these persons, Maslow believed self-actualization could be achieved by all—prince or pauper, Alaskan or African, and, perhaps to some people's surprise, the mother at home.

Therapist Carl Rogers concerns himself with the detours on the path to becoming self-actualized, or "fully functioning," as he calls it. Like Maslow, he believes that self-regard and regard for others must go together. However, a careful study of fully functioning people reveals that they are not driven by personal ambition, for money or extrinsic rewards, but have a genuine concern for the welfare of others. Even Dr. Spock laments the loss of traditional values: "In the past women felt that the family was the most important thing in life, and I myself think that they were correct in that judgment. It's too bad that men didn't adopt that vision. Now many Americans feel that the salary and prestige of the job have the highest priority, and that family life can be sacrificed. People simply don't think of getting gratification from the family anymore—and that, in my opinion, is a great distortion of life.[5]

Characteristics of the "Self-Actualized" Person

* I am realistically oriented. (There are others in the world besides me.)
* I accept myself, others, and the natural world for what they are. (Others have natural needs as powerful as my own.)
* I have a great deal of spontaneity. I am not trying to be anything other than myself. (Implied: I can also accept others as themselves.)
* I am not self-centered; rather I am *problem*-centered. (My needs are no more important than others' needs.)
* I am autonomous and maintain my integrity in the face of opposition and rejection. (I am secure enough to know my own mind and solve my own problems. If there is a problem with others, I will discuss the problem, but maintain my integrity.)
* I value privacy and seek out solitude. (I am *not* aloof. I simply do not value fame and popularity, but enjoy some time alone.)
* My appreciation of people and things is fresh, rather than stereotyped. (Life is different every day, both for others and for me.)
* I do not confuse means with ends. (So that every moment of life is genuine, the *process* of reaching a goal must be as useful as reaching the goal.)
* I have had profound mystical or spiritual experiences. (Communion with my soul is nourishing.)
* I identify with mankind—other human beings, as well as family members. I have close relationships with a few especially loved people. (My intimate relationships with others are profound and deeply emotional, rather than artificial.)

* My values and attitudes are democratic. (Every man's needs are as important as my own.)
* My sense of humor is not hostile or sarcastic, but philosophical. I laugh with people, not at them. (Every person deserves a chance.)
* I resist conformity to culture. (Just because a majority does something doesn't mean it is right for the time or can't be changed.)
* I transcend the environment rather than just cope with it. I approach each day with a "sense of discovery." I am rarely bored because of my ability to appreciate even the simplest thing. (I can appreciate even a child's moment of growth.)[6]

Meeting the Needs of the Individual

Every one of us has a need to feel successful, important, loved, needed, valued, and appreciated. In order to meet our needs for personal significance, we all desire to do something to prove to ourselves and others that we are successful. We fantasize about writing a novel, being president of an organization, or becoming rich or famous. Reality, however, tells us that very few people can obtain this type of fame, fortune, or public acclaim. If everyone did, no one could be of higher status than another and acclaim would lose its appeal to the competitive mind. However, Maslow's self-actualization characteristics can be obtained by everyone, because they are not subject to competition and comparison with others and are open to all, regardless of race, status, sex, or power. Instead, the characteristics of the self-actualized person are ruled by the individual's attitude toward daily living and relationships.

A society in which one has to obtain greater fame, success, and fortune than others in order to be worthwhile can meet the basic psychological needs of only a few.

Individual needs can best be met in small, personal groups that can provide every member with positive regard and support. Here, from the small social group, the individual can find the courage to broaden his or her experience into larger groups such as school, church, city, state, or nation, if desired. But where are these small support groups to be found? They are, of course, families. The individual's goal of self-actualization can be met in the family. The family role and family experience continue to provide the greatest happiness for humanity.

Meeting individual needs in the family—it works! And why does it work? It works because in a family, both mother and father are needed and loved. And they can communicate to each child that he or she is needed and loved. For the self-actualized person who receives life's satisfaction from caring and service, the profession of mother at home becomes meaningful and self-fulfilling. The advantage of this family life system is that everyone can meet basic needs for love, success, and appreciation without competing with others. There is no need for losers. Here every man, woman, and child can become self-actualized.

A world of no losers! That's what returning to a higher set of values through family living can mean for our society. And it is best demonstrated by these mothers who turn their backs on shallow materialism to focus on the values of the natural relationships found in the family. We have already seen that Maslow's self-actualized person has the integrity to answer no to outside pressures, and is not willing to compromise close human relationships. This is the very reason the mother at home is in an excellent position to be self-actualized and become a fully functioning person.

Time for Self-Development

Time has not, historically, been available to either men or women on the large scale that it is for homemakers today. Women can benefit immensely from labor-saving devices and the emerging attitude that it is permissible, desirable, and necessary for men to help more in the home. In contrast, personal time is basically unavailable in the workplace except for short coffee breaks and some limited paid vacations. It would be a tragic loss if the time now being made available to women at home were lost in underpaid and unfulfilling employment. For women today, this is a small window in time that can be used for self-development. And the basic step to accomplishing this self-development is education. Education can and should be synonymous with homemaking.

Education: Essential to Quality Homemaking

We propose that education become closely associated with homemaking. With no change in basic social structure, homemakers can become the most educated group of workers in America. Because of available time, women at home can take advantage of educational opportunities never before accessible to such a large group of adults. The educational level of mothers could exceed that of almost all large social groups. We feel that a high level of education is not only desirable, but necessary for mothers who wish to provide children with optimal, sensitive, and intelligent care in our complex world.

Depending on the phase of a woman's life, she could either jump into education or pursue it an inch at a time. Education can be sought both formally and informally—through community adult education programs, extensions of the public school system, junior colleges and universities, extension centers, home study courses, educational and public television channels (which may have courses available), and the easy access of information in our culture, namely, books and libraries. In most communities there are study groups ranging from art to sciences.

An educated homemaker can reach out to provide service to society in various aspects beyond the family context. We have seen, as our culture has evolved, the rapid increase of women's involvement in politics and other branches of community service. A woman's education increases her concerns for all segments of our society that relate to family. This would include community services that promote the development of individuals. At this point, homemaking will ideally involve activities within the home and outside it, activities that affect the family and social living at all levels. It is through this redefining of homemaking that the myth of homemaking as a dead-end role for women will ultimately be destroyed.

In the meantime, however, no woman who will avail herself of education and the desperate need for social service in our society needs to regard homemaking as uncreative or unfulfilling. There are ample opportunities for service, self-development, and education.

Never before in the history of civilization have so many opportunities for self-development existed for women, particularly women in the home. It may someday be the case that for a mother at home to seek an outside, low-paying job would appear as ludicrous as for an accomplished physician to seek employment as a grocery clerk.

The world for women cannot be improved simply by taking women from the home and placing them in traditional male roles. Women can find new roles, influence, outlets, and creative efforts in the new definitions of the mother role. We see mothers acquiring a larger and larger voice in combatting the adverse influences of society and threats upon children. Femaleness as we know it today, and have recognized it in the past, will emphasize sensitivity, kindness, and wisdom in caring for others—cooperation rather than competition. This female projects the type of image needed in the years ahead. The interaction of the homemaker with the outside world will be one in which homemakers are better compensated for the effort and contribution we give to society. We envision love and personal appreciation as sufficient rewards for our involvements.

In her fact-filled book on the forgotten worker, Rae André states: "My own preference would be to salvage the idea of the home as a place of peace—whether for individuals or for families—and as a physical expression of a person's interest and esthetics and to reject values that make the home a display area for affluence or for the products of creative consuming."[7]

As the homemaker wisely prepares one step at a time, within the seasons of her life, she can and will emerge educated, accomplished, and vital to society. This she will be able to do, not in spite of family and home life, but because of her experience as a mother at home.

MYTH 10

Homemakers Are an Endangered Species

As statistics on the number of employed mothers climb, we read opinions that the mother at home is becoming a woman of the past. Support and appreciation for this natural role are declining simply because people are led to believe that there are more fulfilling roles elsewhere.

Overlooked by many are the mothers who, having taken a place in the work force, are once again returning home. Jan Treinen, a professional woman who returned home, lists commitment to the home, support from her husband, and caring for her children as the reasons she now wants to be home. She says that she recently got a call from her former company and was offered a wonderful job with prestige, a great salary, benefits, and opportunity for advancement. She had left that same company several months earlier to be home with her fifteen-month-old daughter. It had been a difficult decision at the time, and now she was going through it again.

She explains, "My first thoughts were of returning to a 'place' where I could be 'me' again—to make important decisions and (try) to impress important people. . . . I thought how great it would be to get away from crying babies, dirty diapers, and child-related work (I do child care in my home). A second chance. Maybe I could be Supermom, just like everyone else."

Her moment of revelation came quietly. "Then my daughter woke from her nap, her limp little body still warm from sleep. I cradled her in my arms, kissed her forehead, and I knew—there really WAS no decision to be made. There wasn't even a choice. I could not, ever again, leave this special warm moment to anyone else.

"Sound dramatic? It is. It's such a strong emotional tie, such a major commitment, and it comes from the heart. But it's so very real and so very important."[1]

These words capture the essence of a common tug-of-war for the hearts and minds of modern women. From a logical point of view, there are more rewards and a more prestigious life awaiting many women in the marketplace. But the decision must be weighed against the pulls of human nature and the heart.

Commitment Required

Woman like Jan Treinen who are staying home are there because of commitment. Many seem to agree with C. S. Lewis's assessment of the homemaker's role: "It is surely in reality the most important work in the world. What do ships, railways, mines, cars, and governments exist for except that people may be fed, warmed, and safe in their own homes. . . . We wage war in order to have peace, we work in order to have leisure, we produce food in order to eat. So your job is the one for which all others exist."[2] If only society could catch the vision of Lewis's profound and insightful statement! One experienced mother recalls the challenges she had faced when starting out as a young mother. She was struggling with her role when she started to realize that a big part of her problem was that she was trying to succeed without acquiring the extra measures of patience, commitment, unselfishness, and optimism essential for success as a mother. She explains: "This is not a very popular viewpoint in much of the world today, but I believe that a wife and mother will almost surely fail to whatever degree she clings to self-centeredness. I also believe that one reason many women today are tempted to avoid the traditional role is not that the role lacks challenge and opportunity for growth, but rather that it requires *too much* growth. Being successful as a wife and mother and homemaker requires spiritual qualities and attributes of character that do not seem very fashionable to many in this era of me-ism."

Her insights are remarkable, especially in view of the recent change in advice from psychologists. A focus on the self was at first thought to be the way to self-development. But service to others is now being understood as a more sure route to personal growth. The mother at home needs no psychologist to tell her that. One mother of ten was asked which child she loved the most. "I suppose," she smiled, with a twinkle in her eye, "it's the child who is sick or the one away from home . . . the one who needs me the most." Today's mother must know this to survive this world of confusing messages.

A husband's support is not only important, but essential, in helping to establish the rights of his wife to be home. Just as a woman will grow closer to her husband if she can support his role and identify with his work, the husband helps by involving himself in the home and understanding his place there as a father and husband. Janet says: "My husband plays a strong role in the family setting. His organizational skills are greatly needed, as well as time spent with the family and its members. I also involve myself as much as time allows with his activities outside the home. For example, we recently attended a conference where he presented two papers. I always talk to him about his day as he does to me about mine. He learns of the children's needs through my observations and fills in the gaps."

An Attitude Change

In order for women to want to be home, our society must change in attitude. Arlene Cardozo began studying happy mothers when she and her husband moved to Cambridge, Massachusetts, in 1964. The women who enjoyed their young families—who had made a choice of quality family life over the boom of women's lib—she came to call the women of Corine Street. What were they like? Some general characteristics set them apart. First, while they came from a variety of educational backgrounds and work experience, they felt that raising their families was their most important commitment. Second, they did not look upon housework as a major preoccupation. They distinguished between housework and the care of the children. Third, the women were fortunate enough to be within an easy walk to the museums, close to the mainstream of thought and activity. Another important characteristic: their husbands were an integral part of family life. Even though they also had limited budgets, crowded conditions, and high-pressure work situations for husbands, the husbands' emphasis was on high-quality family life.[3]

This same author helped coordinate a Harvard newcomers' organization, and continued investigating the factors that contribute to a woman's enjoyment of being at home. She compared the attitudes of women who were happy at home with feelings of those who were not. Most of the several hundred women from various parts of the country affiliated with the newcomers' program were raising families. Some, like the women of Corine Street, enjoyed being at home, while others viewed themselves as "trapped housewives." What made the difference?

Cardozo concluded: "One sharp contrast was that the woman who enjoyed being at home used her ingenuity and creativity to retain existing interests or to develop new ones while at home, but the woman who was unhappy at home often could not function productively away from school or office without someone else to give her assignments and deadlines. It never occurred to her to find new ways to use her abilities, if being at home precluded her doing things in old ways. Nor did she develop new interests if old ones couldn't fit into her new routine."[4]

Moreover, the woman happy at home did not consider herself a "housekeeper," while the discontented woman almost always cited housework as an overwhelming and prime complaint, feeling that "housekeeper" was her prime occupation.

The more Cardozo talked with women about what determined enjoyment and satisfaction at home, as opposed to boredom and loneliness, the more apparent it became that the woman who enjoyed being at home had consciously decided to be there and had definite goals. Dissatisfied women often felt that their positions were forced on them by society; others felt their husbands wanted them at home. Along with the feeling that she was forced, the dissatisfied woman did not have a vision of what she hoped to accomplish with her family.[5]

Social Attitudes and Aspirations

Attitudes, not statistics, will ultimately add credibility to the durability of homemakers—and social attitudes among young women indicate that they still aspire to and value the homemaker's role. For example, in a 1976 study, 52 percent of a sample of young married women and 63 percent of their husbands agreed with the statement that the "wife should work only if it does not interfere with household responsibilities." In the same sample, 60 percent and 82 percent also agreed with the statement: "If there are young children, the wife should not work unless there are serious financial needs."[6] Is it possible to establish a society based on these aspirations rather than social policy and projections of statistical trends?

In a study indicating a trend to delay parenthood, it was found that parenthood was seen as a desirable role by the majority of 213 students in a large Midwestern university. Among these students, most indicated that a two-child family was closest to the ideal family, and childlessness was selected by only 3.3 percent.[7]

Why We Do What We Do

We can't ignore the driving factor of why most women are at home. Author Rae André clarifies a key point in her book, *Homemakers: The Forgotten Workers*: "Ask an American homemaker what she does, and she is likely to say she takes care of her children and her husband and her home. Ask her why she does these things, and she is likely to say she does them mostly out of *love*."[8]

Although women often fail to feel supported in the most challenging and consuming role ever undertaken, they "hang in there" and will continue to do so. Why? Because they love "at-home" relationships, and find fulfillment in their role.

Emerging Mother Support Groups

One of the new women's movements currently emerging is the network of support groups among women who choose to stay at home rather than seek employment outside the home. The rapid emergence of these support groups was the focus of an article appearing in 1985 in the *Wall Street Journal*: "To help draw mothers and their infants out of isolation, family centers have developed several techniques. (The Family Resource Coalition, based in Chicago, maintains the most complete lists of centers.)

"The Mothers' Center, for example, blends child-care with social activism. This nationwide network of 33 centers forms, among other things, 'committees' of about 10 mothers who meet once a week to tackle local issues. In 1974, the first Mothers' Center, a group in Hicksville, New York, persuaded a local hospital to allow fathers into the labor room. More recently, another group petitioned its town library to drop its ban on baby strollers.

"In New York, the 92nd Street YM-YWHA offers 'Park Bench for Mothers,' a weekly play and talk group. In Grand Rapids, Mich., Parents Supporting Parents, Inc. focuses on helping women through the first six months of motherhood. In Eugene, Ore., Birth to Three Inc. organizes neighborhood groups that meet in participants' homes. The approximately 55 groups now in operation aren't intended solely to help stay-at-home mothers, says Andi Fischhoff, a cofounder, but they do address their problems. 'There's so much emphasis on women working that the woman staying at home feels forgotten,' she says."[9]

Why Is the Full-Time Homemaker Here to Stay?

It is the basic nature of the woman to yearn to care for and guide her family in her home. Women in other cultures who have stepped into a more "equalized" employment role have soon realized the disadvantages and later desired to be home with their families. Even in communal situations, women seek the children.

Also, many young American families have chosen to keep the mother in the home even when their lives are put at an economic disadvantage. Why do they choose this lifestyle, even at a financial sacrifice? Lecturer Sharlene Bartholomew tells of riding across a university campus in a shuttle and hearing two young women suggest that the big difference in today's society is that young mothers *have* to work just to pay rent, whereas in the past it was easier for the woman to remain home full-time. After they got out, the shuttle driver commented, "Don't put too much stock in what they said. It can be done. My wife does stay home with our baby while I'm in school. But we are *so* poor." Here is a couple that realizes where true riches lie.

Because of the great value of homemakers to our society, we propose that society recognize their worth and work to improve the conditions of women, not neglect them.

There is truly a "silent majority" of women who seek support to improve the status and condition of their role.

Rather than eliminate the homemaker option so that women in greater numbers can seek equality in social, often male-preferred roles, we should seek to change public attitudes so the mother-homemaker can "feel" equal and necessary to society. Anne Barash, a professional woman from Syracuse, New York, explains this concept in her letter to all mothers at home, printed in *Welcome Home*. After expressing appreciation to stay-at-home moms for their involvement in school and child-oriented clubs, as well as their wisdom in behalf of children, she continues, "We most admire your courage in living your life in accordance with the values of motherhood such as loving, caring, and giving. Those of us who have stayed at home and left also admire the incredible self-discipline which enables you to work at a job that is 24 hours a day, which has no defined tasks, and which doesn't compensate you with yearly salary increases, paid vacations, sick days, or holidays. . . .

"Finally, we hope that someday we can return a few of the favors you've done for us and that when your children leave home, you'll share with the rest of the world some of the special talents that only full-time stay-at-home mothers possess. It is important to all of us, as people, that we recognize the essential contribution that your work makes to our world."[10]

Our goal in writing this book has been to improve the status of mothers at home and gain support for their ever-challenging and fulfilling role. We contend that the myth "homemakers are an endangered species" will itself become obsolete. As long as there is the need to nurture, comfort, and sustain life, the mother at home will endure and hold on to her birthright.

Notes

Myth 1

1. Anne Oakley, *Woman's Work: The Housewife Past and Present* (New York: Random House, 1976), p. 233.

2. Letter to author, 1985. See also Linda Burton, Cheri Loveless, et al. (Washington, D. C.: Acropolis, 1986).

3. Benjamin Beit-Hallahmi and Albert I. Rabin, "The Kibbutz as a Social Experiment and as a Child-Rearing Laboratory," *American Psychologist* 32 (July 1977): 532–41.

4. Hedrick Smith, *The Russians* (New York: Times Books, 1983), p. 136.

5. Fox Butterfield, *China: Alive in the Bitter Sea* (New York: Times Books, 1982), pp. 172–73.

6. Alice Rossi, "Gender and Parenthood," *American Sociological Review* 49 (February 1984):8.

7. Betty Friedan, *The Second Stage* (New York: Summit Books, 1981), pp. 340–41.

8. Letter to author.

9. Arlene R. Cardozo, *Woman at Home* (Garden City, NY: Doubleday, 1976), p. 9.

10. Jan A. Treinen, *Welcome Home*, September 1985, p. 28.

Myth 2

1. Pam Svoboda, "I'm Not the Person I Was," *Welcome Home*, January 1986, p. 21.

2. Deborah Fallows, *A Mother's Work* (Boston: Houghton-Mifflin, 1985), p. 16.

3. Ibid., p. 231.

4. Nachman, Pat, Conversation with author at the Parenting Studies Symposium held in Chicago, 1984.

5. "Speaker Praises Chimps as Humans' Mirror," *Salt Lake Tribune*, April 29, 1986, B:3.

6. Sterling G. Ellsworth and Richard G. Ellsworth, *Getting to Know the Real You* (Salt Lake City: Deseret Book, 1980), pp. 153-54.

7. Fallows, *A Mother's Work*, p. 230.

Myth 3

1. Raymond Montemayor and Mark D. Clayton, "Maternal Employment and Adolescent Development," *Theory into Practice* 22 (Spring 1983):117.

2. Edward M. Levine, "The Middle-Class Family and Middle-Class Adolescents in a State of Disarray: A Social-Psychiatric Analysis," *Psychiatry* 47 (May 1984):160.

3. Larry Jensen and Marilyn Borges, "The Effect of Maternal Employment on Adolescent Daughters," *Adolescence*, in press.

4. Larry Jensen and Janet Jensen, "Maternal Employment: A Closer Look at a No-Difference Conclusion," *Parenting Studies*, in press.

5. Harry Stein, "The Case For Staying at Home," *Esquire*, June 1984, pp. 142, 144.

6. Lee Salk, as quoted in Stein, p. 149.

7. William and Wendy Dreskin, as quoted in Stein, p. 148.

Myth 4

1. Personal conversation with author.

2. Deborah Fallows, *A Mother's Work* (Boston: Houghton-Mifflin, 1985), p. 13.

3. Ibid., pp. 126–27.

4. Joan Beck, "Mom's Time: Too Important to Waste on Kids," *Denver Post*, April 18, 1982, C-48.

5. Amitai Etzioni, "U.S. needs a 'moral and social recovery,' " *U.S. News and World Report* 96 (Jan. 9, 1984):60.

6. Karla C. Erickson, *Take Time to Smell the Dandelions* (Salt Lake City: Bookcraft, 1979), p. 1.

7. Fallows, *A Mother's Work*, p. 16.

Myth 5

1. Arlene R. Cardozo, *Woman at Home* (Garden City, N.Y.: Doubleday, 1976), pp. 13–14.

2. Ibid.

3. Cardozo, pp. 17–19.

4. Ibid., p. 21.

5. James E. Faust, "A Message to Our Granddaughters," *BYU Speeches of the Year*, 1984–85, p. 79.

6. Sara Davidson, "Having It All," *Esquire*, June 1984, pp. 54–60.

7. Ibid.

8. Harry Stein, "The Case for Staying at Home," *Esquire*, June 1984, p. 147.

9. Karla C. Erickson, *Take Time to Make Time Count* (Salt Lake City: Bookcraft, 1984), pp. 77–79.

Myth 6

1. Bonnie Siverd, *Family Circle*, March 1986.

2. Alan Furst, "The Golden Age of Goo: How Debbi and Randy Fields Unleashed a Cookie Monster," *Esquire*, December 1984, pp. 326, 330.

3. Mary Jane Magdanz, "A Dollar Saved," *Welcome Home*, February 1986, pp. 26, 30.

4. Christopher Turner, "Dual-Work Households and Marital Dissolution," *Human Relations* 24 (December 1971):535–48.

5. Carin Rubenstein, "Real Men Don't Earn Less Than Their Wives," *Psychology Today* 16 (November 1982):36–41.

6. Marianne A. Ferber and Bonnie G. Birnbaum, "Economics of the Family: Who Maximizes Well," *Family Economics Review*, Summer/Fall 1980, p. 15.

7. Joseph H. Pleck, Graham L. Stains, and Linda Lang, "Conflicts between Work and Family Life," *Monthly Labor Review* 103 (March 1980):30.

8. John G. Condron and Jerry G. Bode, "Working Wives, and Family Division of Labor: Middletown, 1980," *Journal of Marriage and the Family* 44 (May 1982): 421–26.

9. John Scanzoni and Greer Litton Fox, "Sex Roles, Family and Society: The Seventies and Beyond," *Journal of Marriage and the Family* 42 (November 1980):743–56.

10. Edward P. Lazear and Robert T. Michael, "Real Income Equivalence Among One-Earner and Two-Earner Families," *American Economic Review* 70 (May 1980):203–8.

11. Frank D. Cox, *Human Intimacy: Marriage, the Family and Its Meaning* (St. Paul: West Publishing, 1984), pp. 272–75.

12. Barbara B. Smith, *The Love That Never Faileth* (Salt Lake City: Bookcraft, 1984), pp. 138–39.

Myth 7

1. E. E. LeMasters and John DeFrain, *Parents in Contemporary America: A Sympathetic View*, 4th ed. (Homewood, IL: Dorsey Press, 1983), p. 155.

2. A. Regula Herzog, Jerald G. Bachman, and Lloyd D. Johnston, "Paid Work, Child Care, and Housework: A National

Survey of High School Seniors' Preferences for Sharing Responsibilities between Husband and Wife," *Sex Roles* 9 (January 1983):109–34.

3. Jean Atkinson and Ted L. Huston, "Sex Role Orientation and Division of Labor Early in Marriage," *Journal of Personality and Social Psychology* 46 (February 1984):330–45.

4. Linda Nyquist et al., "Household Responsibilities in Middle-Class Couples: The Contribution of Demographic and Personality Variables," *Sex Roles* 12 (January 1985):15–34.

5. Peter J. Stein, "Men in Families," *Marriage and Family Review* 7 (Fall/Winter 1984):143–62.

6. Arlene R. Cardozo, *Woman at Home* (Garden City, NY: Doubleday, 1976), p. 147.

7. Deborah Fallows, *A Mother's Work* (Boston: Houghton Mifflin, 1985), p. 45.

8. Ibid., p. 46.

Myth 8

1. Rae André, *Homemakers: The Forgotten Workers* (Chicago: University of Chicago Press, 1981), p. 225.

2. Hamilton I. McCubbin and Barbara Blum Dahl, *Marriage and Family: Individuals and Life Cycles* (New York: John Wiley & Sons, 1985), p. 357.

3. Kathleen Slaugh Bahr, "More Than Clean Windows: The Unrecognized Value of Housework," *Ensign* 15 (October 1985):60–64.

4. André, p. 225.

5. *Chartbook*, U.S. Department of Labor, Bureau of Statistics (1983).

6. Doris Lund, "Pardon Me, But I LIKE Housework," *Reader's Digest* 125 (December 1984):213–16.

7. Daryl V. Hoole, *The Art of Homemaking* (Salt Lake City: Deseret Book, 1969), pp. 136–37.

8. Dorothy Lee, as quoted in Bahr, pp. 60–61.

9. Hoole, pp. 12, 14.

Myth 9

1. Barbara Kantrowitz et al., "A Mother's Choice," *Newsweek*, March 31, 1986, p. 49.

2. Linda Burton, as quoted in "Group Boosts Mothers Who Stay at Home," *Washington Post*, May 10, 1984, B-23.

3. Michael A. Wallach and Lise Wallach, *Psychology's Sanction for Selfishness: The Error of Egoism in Theory and Therapy* (New York: W. H. Freeman, 1983), p. 229.

4. Urie Bronfenbrenner, "The Disturbing Changes in the American Family," *American Family*, February 1977, p. 24.

5. Benjamin Spock, as quoted in Carol Pogash, "What Every Working Mother Must Know," *Redbook*, October 1984, p. 28.

6. Abraham Maslow, *Motivation and Personality* (New York: Harper & Row, 1970), pp. 149–74.

7. Rae André, *Homemakers: The Forgotten Workers* (Chicago: University of Chicago Press, 1981), p. 64.

Myth 10

1. Jan A. Treinen, *Welcome Home*, February 1986, p. 32.

2. As quoted in Barbara B. Smith, *The Love That Never Faileth* (Salt Lake City: Bookcraft, 1984), p. 178.

3. Arlene R. Cardozo, *Woman at Home* (Garden City, NY: Doubleday, 1976), p. 10.

4. Ibid., p. 11.

5. Ibid., p. 10.

6. Marianne A. Ferber, "Labor Market Participation of Young Married Women: Causes and Effects," *Journal of Marriage and the Family* 44 (May 1982):457–67.

7. Patricia K. Kanaub, Deanna B. Eversoll, and Jacqueline H. Voss, "Is Parenthood a Desirable Adult Role? An Assessment of Attitudes Held by Contemporary Women," *Sex Roles* 9 (March 1981):355–61.

8. Rae André, *Homemakers: The Forgotten Workers* (Chicago: University of Chicago Press, 1981), p. 41. Emphasis added.

9. "New Minority of Mothers at Home Finds Support in Family Centers," *Wall Street Journal*, October 25, 1985, p. 33.

10. Anne Barash, *Welcome Home*, December 1985, p. 32.

Index